Come, Walk With Me

POEMS, DEVOTIONALS, AND SHORT WALKS
AMONG PLEASANT PEOPLE AND PLACES

Come, Walk With Me

POEMS, DEVOTIONALS, AND SHORT WALKS
AMONG PLEASANT PEOPLE AND PLACES

Come, Walk With Me

POEMS, DEVOTIONALS, AND SHORT WALKS
AMONG PLEASANT PEOPLE AND PLACES

ELWOOD McQUAID

The Friends of Israel Gospel Ministry, Inc.
P. O. Box 908, Bellmawr, NJ 08099

Come, Walk With Me

POEMS, DEVOTIONALS, AND SHORT WALKS
AMONG PLEASANT PEOPLE AND PLACES

Copyright © 1990
The Friends of Israel Gospel Ministry, Inc.
Bellmawr, New Jersey 08099

First Edition 1990

Cover photo—Winterthur Gardens, Wilmington, DE
© H. Armstrong Roberts

Printed in the United States of America
Library of Congress Catalog Card Number 89-82580
I.S.B.N. 0-915540-47-9

Table of Contents

Introduction

You will not learn a great many new things by reading this book—more knowledge is not the goal. *Come, Walk With Me* is offered, rather, in the spirit of Samuel Johnson who believed "that people more often need to be reminded than informed." Being reminded, I think, is the simplest and best antidote for the discouragement so many Christians are experiencing today. Discouragement isolates, intimidates, and, if allowed to go unchecked, eventually devastates the life and testimony of the believer. Our design is, at least in some measure, to help liberate those who are in need of some cheerful reminders.

Poems, people, and pleasant places will converge as we pursue our objective.

Those of you who have read *Words Along the Way* will recognize a few of the poems. I have included in this volume some which have ministered most effectively, "Death Meets the Master" among them.

Twenty-seven poems in the first section are based on events from the life of our Lord recorded in the Gospel records, a beginning to a project I hope will eventually encompass every significant event in the four Gospels. Each poem or essay will provide the basis for a devotional retreat or further Bible study. And while retracing our Lord's footsteps and the experiences of the ones He touched, we will be reminded to claim the treasures we possess in Christ.

To satisfy frequent requests for more information about the illustrious black preacher, John Jasper, I have included a short biography, "Go, Tell'em John." Stonewall Jackson admirers will find a companion piece, "Stonewall Jackson's Bible," detailing God's working in the life of a Civil War contemporary of Jasper's who was on the other side of the color line.

We'll pass through old graveyards—read an epitaph or two as we pass—up mountain peaks, along garden rows, across verdant farm meadows, down lonely roads, and sit for a while beside a quiet New England pond. On our brief trip to the Middle East we'll stroll along the streets of Old Jerusalem among animated Israelis, scale Masada's serpentine path, and climb to Mount Calvary's summit. Patriots, founding fathers, and boys in blue and gray all have something to say to us. We'll romp with grandkids a bit before I introduce some people who have profoundly marked my life for God. Finally, we'll scurry up the hollows of rural Kentucky and have a good time with Pastor Frank and Ned Arbuckle as they create an ill-fated "Christmas in July."

The great thing about this trip is you can take it from a sickbed, shut-in's room, jail cell, den, folding chair at the beach, or any place big enough to allow holding a book in your hand. If you decide to go, I know you'll enjoy it.

Come, walk with me!

Come, Walk With Me

Come, walk with me along the way,
Let's see what we can see
Around the bend, across the hills
Where birds fly wild and free.

Perhaps we'll venture to the sea
And watch ships pass the shore,
See them float on billowed sail
Beyond the breaker's roar.

Or would you like to board a plane
To give the winds a run?
Look on as snowy castles rise
Majestic in the sun.

But when we've looked at everything
And roamed the whole world wide,
The best of it will still be this:
We've done it side by side.

In The Beginning
John 1:1–14

"In the beginning"—**God was**
  In pristine realms of His eternity.

"In the beginning"—**Time was**
  Created by His Word and measured by a
    planet's track around one blazing star.

"In the beginning"—**Man was**
  Born of mud and Yahweh's Spirit breath.

"In the beginning"—**Sin was**
  And sullied mankind's infant innocence.

"In the beginning"—**The Word was**
  "And the Word became flesh, and dwelt
    among us . . ."

. . . and so it all began.

Nazareth
Luke 1:26–37

*And in the sixth month the angel, Gabriel, was sent from God
unto a city in Galilee, named Nazareth* (v. 26).

Gabriel coming here?
You must be mad!
Or could it be that
He has lost his way?
Jerusalem's the proper
Place for him—
Even sage and priest
Avoid our town.

No, angels go where
God directs their way
Unerringly to find
The favored ones.
His business now
Is not on Temple Mount,
Nor where the ring of
Rabbi's voice is heard.
But rather he converses
With a maid,
And stands in sawdust
With a carpenter.

Mary
Luke 1:27–56

And Mary said, Behold the handmaid of the Lord; be it unto me according to thy word (v. 38).

Galilee was clean and green,
    and so was she—
Lovely, like spring flowers
    before the breeze.

Virgin maid unschooled
    in baser things,
With heart toward God
    that leaped up for His Word.

This was Mary,
    "handmaid of the Lord,"
Frail little temple
    born to bear our King.

She didn't know the heights
    to which she'd soar,
Nor how a cruel sword
    would pierce her soul.

Joseph
Matthew 1:18–25

Joseph, thou son of David, fear not to take unto thee Mary, thy wife; for that which is conceived in her is of the Holy Spirit. And she shall bring forth a son, and thou shalt call his name JESUS; for he shall save his people from their sins (vv. 20–21).

Godly, sensitive and very
Much in love
Was Joseph, the village
Carpenter of Nazareth.
Tormented now, he pondered
Mary's state—
Found with child before
They shared a marriage bed.

Hold her up to public ridicule?
No, never that.
A quiet termination was
The way to minimize
The shame that soiled
The girl.

Then God sent down the
Angel of the Lord
With explanations
For his troubled mind.
"Fear not," the settling word
That came to him—
Heaven was conducting this affair

Spirit, prophet's word,
And virgin fair
Had all converged
To bring the thing to pass
Immanuel was coming to
Earth's vale,
And Joseph would stand vigil
At His birth.

His Little Remnant

The second chapter of Luke's Gospel draws together a series of portraits of the Lord's expectant remnant—those who were looking and longing for the Messiah's appearance.

Readers are transported across events spanning 12 years of Jesus' early life in an exhilarating panorama that sweeps down from Heaven past caroling angels, over the shepherds' fields, into the stable at Bethlehem, up to the Temple Mount, through the courts of the sanctuary, away into Galilee and Nazareth, then back to Jerusalem again.

The Savior is surrounded by Mary, Joseph, wondering shepherds, prophesying Simeon, thankful Anna, kinfolk, acquaintances, and astonished teachers of the Law.

While angelic emissaries fulfill their mission, the Holy Spirit, Father, and, of course, the Son are set forth in the diverse aspects of their ministries: the Son's coming, the Spirit's enlightening, and the Father's plan being pursued.

Through it all, there is a magnificent intimacy which seems to usher reverent observers into an inner sanctuary of divine companionship and communication. It is a rewarding experience to walk slowly—ever so slowly—through this chapter.

It is significant, I think, that the Holy Spirit seems to purposefully display, so early and emphatically, that little band of saints who, above all things in life, awaited His coming into the world. Indeed, He seems to take special care in showing us the remnant before the rebels are allowed on the scene.

This should cause us to pause and consider something worthy of comment. I don't know how it is with you, but I often find myself giving far too much of my thought life and conversation to unpleasant people who do equally unpleasant things. I have known Christians who are defeated and embittered by that rebel band who seems to find a sadistic kind of pleasure in dividing saints, while destroying churches in the process.

It would, it seems, be in order to reverse the pattern by fixing our thoughts on those warm and godly brothers and sisters in Christ, loving encouragers, who want to help us on with the Lord. They are all about us, and your life and mine are being touched continually by this faithful remnant.

Let us be thankful for them, tell them so, and ask God to give us like ministry toward them.

Just Another Baby Boy?

And when he had gathered all the chief priests and scribes of the people together, he demanded of them where the Christ should be born. And they said to him, In Bethlehem of Judea; for thus it is written by the prophet,

**And thou Bethlehem, in the land of Judah,
art not the least among the princes of Judah;
for out of thee shall come a Governor
that shall rule my people, Israel (Mt. 2:4-6).**

Just another baby boy
   Born in Bethlehem town.
One more hungry mouth to feed,
   And so the world slept on.
It was a weary, captive world
   Gripped tight in Rome's domain.
The chilling fear of tyranny
   Fast held them like a chain.
Another baby, more or less,
   What difference could He be?
One more soul to bear the pain
   And share their misery.
So passed mankind a winter's night,
   Those beaten down by sin,
Too dull to hear angelic strains
   That rose above the din.

Near two millennia have passed
   Since God took human frame.
The world runs its appointed course,
   But nevermore the same.
He gathered up the captive's chain
   Once forged for you and me.
He broke the foul tyrant's grasp
   And purchased liberty.

Now looms above the manger bed
   A message for all men:
He died; He lives; He intercedes;
   He's coming back again!
Then herald forth the joyous word,
   Our voices lift as one,
The Babe who slept in cattle stall
   Is God's triumphant Son.

Who Is He?

And they came with haste, and found Mary, and Joseph, and the babe lying in a manger (Lk. 2:16).

Who is this whose entrance was with dazzling light
    and angels' symphony?
And why stand we in company with startled beasts
    while He serenely sleeps on matted hay?
What has He come here for? Tiny one adored by mother's
    gaze and rustic shepherd band.

He's all that God would send for you and me,
    The sum of every prophet's "saith the Lord."
    Immanuel, with "healing in His wings" for every
        sin-struck son of Adam's kind.

He's all we need.
    Come down to save our souls, then lift us high above
        the mournful sounds of death throes rising from a
            stricken world to join with those of royal heritage—
                "Heirs of God," and "Children of the Light."

He's all in all.
    And one day soon, His promises all kept—the lambs all
        in and resting at His side—we'll sing of Him
    who entered by a stall: Worthy is our God to reign supreme!

The Dedication
Luke 2:21-24

And when the days of her purification according to the law of Moses were accomplished, they brought him to Jerusalem, to present him to the Lord (v. 22).

They took the infant Jesus
 "To present Him to the Lord."
Up to Old Jerusalem,
 Obeying Moses' word.

A proper sacrifice was carried
 To a Temple room,
As must be done for "every male
 That openeth the womb."

Turtledoves and pigeons,
 The poorest of the poor.
It was the best the couple had,
 What could they offer more?

Him and themselves they offered,
 Which was a better thing
Than any oxen, lamb, or bird
 A worshiper can bring.

Old Simeon
Luke 2:25-35

Lord, now lettest thou thy servant depart in peace, according to
thy word; For mine eyes have seen thy salvation (vv. 29-30).

His life turned on a promise from the Lord:
    He would not die until he'd seen the Christ.
And every sunrise shone upon a question:
    "Will I look into His face today?"
His query fled with the crimson sunset
    The day he took the Babe up in his arms.
At last—at last—he could "depart in peace,"
    And carry on his journey a word to light the way:
"My eyes have seen Thy salvation."
    Old Simeon's lamp still sends its beam away
For those who live in darkness near and far.
    "A light of revelation to the Gentiles," shines the phrase,
"And the glory of Thy people Israel."

Anna
Luke 2:36-38

And there was one Anna, a prophetess, the daughter of Phanuel, of the tribe of Asher; she was of a great age, and had lived with an husband seven years from her virginity; And she was a widow of about fourscore and four years, who departed not from the temple, but served God with fastings and prayers night and day (vv. 36-37).

She was old, this Anna;
   A full eighty years and four,
Waiting in the Temple
   For what God had in store.
She'd witnessed worlds of history,
   May have seen the Romans come to town,
Pompey and his swaggering legionnaries,
   Swords blood-wet from Jews they had cut down.
She'd heard the wails coming from the Temple,
   When pagan feet defiled the holy hill.
Her face tear stained, her breast charged with a question:
   "How could this ever be Jehovah's will?"
Now in those hallowed Temple courts
   She lingered night and day,
Familiar figure known to all
   Who saw her pause and pray.
Her voice rang with thanksgiving
   For His mercy, love, and grace.
She found it all while looking
   Upon the infant's face.
She'd tell all those who waited too
   About the promised one.
He had arrived to touch their lives—
   The everlasting Son.

Herod and the Magi
Matthew 2:1–23

Then Herod, when he had privately called the wise men, inquired of them diligently what time the star appeared. And he sent them to Bethlehem, and said, Go and search diligently for the young child; and when ye have found him, bring me word again, that I may come and worship him also (vv. 7-8).

Crafty Herod was distressed
 At what came to his ear.
Wise men tracked an eastern star,
 And it had led them here.

"Just where will the Christ be born?"
 He queried priests and scribes.
"Bethl'em–Judah, prophet's say,
 Least of Israel's tribes."

"When you've found Him quickly come,"
 A smiling Herod purred.
"I'll join in humble worship there,
 When I receive your word."

Magi knelt before the Babe,
 Presenting treasures rare.
Gold, frankincense, and myrrh
 They placed before Him there.

"Don't go back," the word from God,
 "Depart another way.
Herod's black heart only seeks
 The Child to find and slay."

"Kill them all," the tyrant raves—
 So Bethlehem's babes he slaughters.
Wailing rends the purple night
 From Rachel's stricken daughters.

Far from that depressing scene
   The God-Child finds His bed.
Down in Egypt they will wait
   For word the king is dead.

Herod's soul leaped into hell,
   His infamy was done.
Jehovah's word would now prevail,
   "From Egypt comes my Son."

Jesus With the Rabbis
Luke 2:39-52

And it came to pass that, after three days, they found him in the temple, sitting in the midst of the teachers, both hearing them, and asking them questions (v. 46).

Wise beyond His years, the sages thought,
    and stroked their beards while mulling what he asked.
Only twelve?
Then how is it He knows to say such things?
He's not high-born, that's plain enough to see.
How one so young could know so much of God,
    they'd ponder it while on their beds this night.

Next day—

Jesus' parents burst into the circle.
Their looks of anguish mingled with relief.
"Why have you done this?" they wanted to know.
"We've worried ourselves sick looking for you."
"The Father's business kept me here," He said.
Theirs not to worry, all was well in hand.
And so it was, He and the rabbis parted company,
But one day they would hear from Him again.

Jesus and the Children
Matthew 18:1-6

At the same time came the disciples unto Jesus, saying, Who is the greatest in the kingdom of heaven? And Jesus called a little child unto him, and set him in the midst of them, And said, Verily I say unto you, Except ye be converted, and become as little children, ye shall not enter into the kingdom of heaven (vv. 1-3).

> Little hands around His fingers,
> Little hearts pressed to His chest,
> Little faces up against His cheek
> **—And so His love flowed out to them.**

> "Let them come to me,"
> "Let them learn of me,"
> "Let them trust in me"
> **—And so His words call out to us.**

> A child will show the way to faith,
> A child will lead you to still waters,
> A child will help you find the Kingdom
> **—And so His salvation reaches us.**

The Disciple
Mark 3:19

And he goeth up into a mountain, and called unto him whom he would: and they came unto him (v. 13).

Should I be like Peter,
Full of fire and storm?
Or maybe patient Andrew
With heart for souls so warm?
Surely not a Judas;
No doubting Thomas I.
Perhaps rock–solid Matthew
I could be by and by.
Or what of James and John,
Faithful sons of Zebedee?
Oh, no, He made me what I am;
I'm willing to be me!

On the Mountain
Mark 9:1–10

And after six days Jesus taketh with him Peter, and James, and John, and leadeth them up into an high mountain, apart by themselves; and he was transfigured before them (v. 2).

They climbed up to a mountain peak;
    It rose up like a tower.
In this place they would all behold
    God's Kingdom come with power.

Showing forth His glory,
    White as snow, He did appear.
Babbled they some stumbling words
    To cover for their fear.

Moses and Elijah came
    To talk of His decease,
Of Kingdom's dawn when righteousness
    With knowledge will increase.

Peter thought to be up there
    Was very good indeed.
James and John with whirling minds
    And surging hearts agreed.

"This is my beloved Son."
    The voice came from a cloud.
"Hear Him!" was the terse command
    That echoed long and loud.

Suddenly, they saw no man,
    But looked around to see
Only Jesus and themselves
    In silent company.

Just Jesus and the royal word,
    They later would recall.
"Hear Him!" was not for them alone.
    He says it to us all.

Someday
John 5:1-16

Now there is at Jerusalem, by the sheep gate, a pool, which is called in the Hebrew tongue Bethesda, having five porches. In these lay a multitude of impotent folk, of blind, lame, paralyzed, waiting for the moving of the water (vv. 2-3).

Thirty-eight years he'd waited for his *someday* to arrive.
Must have thought it never would while he was still alive.
He occupied a tattered mat in a place for hopeless cases.
Searched in vain for comfort as he pled with passing faces.
"Come and help an old man to the waters," he would call.
"Don't have time," their looks replied, if, indeed, they looked at all.
His *someday* came on Sabbath morn in form quite unexpected.
No hand to guide him to the pool, just simple words projected.
"It must be mockery," he thought; "so cruel to hear such talk,"
When a Galilean mouth spoke out: "Take up your bed and walk!"
But surging life electrified those limbs of wasted clay.
He leaped to shout for all to hear, "My *someday's* here to stay."

A Boy's Lunch
John 6:1-15

There is a lad here, who hath five barley loaves and two small fishes; but what are they among so many? (v. 9).

He must have been quite a boy
    to part company with his lunch
        without prospects for something better.
Oh, it was rough fare—boney little fish,
    and biscuits fashioned with course barley flour.
He didn't have an inkling of what his selfless
    deed held in store when he told Andrew:
        "He can have my lunch."
It seems quite natural for small boys
    to want to give things to Jesus, millions
        of them have given Him their lives.
He must have been wide-eyed when he saw
    what the Lord did with it—brimming
        baskets moving through the crowd.
Had I been there, I would have sought him out
    to say, "Good for you, lad. You've done a
        wonderful thing today."
It wouldn't have meant much to him, I'm sure,
    but it would have been immensely good for me.

When Jairus' Daughter Died
Mark 5:21–43

*And, behold, there cometh one of the rulers of the synagogue,
Jairus by name; and when he saw him, he fell at his feet, And
besought him greatly, saying, My little daughter lieth at the point of
death. I pray thee, come and lay thy hands on her, that she may be
healed; and she shall live (vv. 22-23).*

Jairus ruled a synagogue
   Where people came to pray.
But he had no voice in Death's affairs—
   His daughter died one day.

A shattered father pleaded,
   "My little daughter's dying.
Come and lay Your hands on her;
   I'll show you where she's lying."

"Too late," they said, "the girl is dead.
   Why trouble you the Master?"
So numb with grief, he set himself
   To grapple with disaster.

"Be not afraid," was Jesus' word.
"It is no time for weeping.
She is not dead," the Savior said,
   "Your child is only sleeping."

He took a little hand in His,
   And told her to arise.
Disciples watched in wonderment
   As light danced in her eyes.

Jairus thanked his God that night,
   For she had life and breath.
He ruled one simple synagogue,
   But Jesus ruled o'er Death!

My Name Is Legion
Luke 8:26-39

*And when he went forth to the land, there met him out of the city
a certain man, who had demons for a long time, and wore no
clothes, neither abode in any house, but in the tombs (v. 27).*

A crazy man—beside himself—
A present danger too.
Guard, chain, and shackle warned
That it was surely true.
A demon legion rampaged through
The caverns of his mind.
Naked, raving midst the tombs,
More beast than humankind.
Jesus sent a question
To pierce his trembling frame.
The first step on his road back home:
"Man, tell me, what's your name?"
"Legion," was the stark reply,
For demons had control.
"Give us pigs as habitat,
If you plan to make him whole."
Pigs it was, and down they ran
To leap into the sea.
While clothed, serene, and at His feet
The man sat demon-free.
But irony of ironies
In what the people do.
They join the demon legion
By choosing swineherd too!
"Go away," they shouted.
"Pig killer, leave this place."
They had no thought for their own kind,
That one so touched by grace.
Things haven't really changed today,
The question's just as big
For those bound by possessions:
"Will it be Christ, or pig?"

The Funeral
Luke 7:11–17

And he came and touched the bier; and they that bore him stood still. And he said, Young man, I say unto thee, Arise. And he that was dead sat up, and began to speak. And he delivered him to his mother (vv. 14-15).

Death and Jesus never were fit companions. As a matter of fact, Death fell into a habit of leaving whenever Jesus came into his presence.

They say he leaped from a casket outside the little village of Nain when Jesus placed His hand on the coffin of a widow's boy.

He ran from a room one day up in Capernaum where he had held a twelve-year-old girl captive for but an hour.

And there was that time in Bethany when, with all of the enemies of Jesus pulling for him, he had to turn Lazarus loose and step aside to let him leave the grave.

When Jesus was about 33, they met on a little hill outside the old city of Jerusalem. Death tried his best to force a reconciliation that time. But Jesus would have none of it, and, after three days, He ordered him out of the tomb.

Paul says his sting is gone. Says he's running kind of an escort service now. He's helping world-weary Christians fold the little tents they've lived in down here then turning them over to the angels for the trip to Heaven.

He'll come for me one day—maybe soon. But when he finds out Jesus lives here, he won't stay around—just long enough to set my spirit free and let me get on home.

The Home at Bethany
John 12:1-11

A well-known Bible teacher was once asked if he would consider doing family life conferences. "I'll be happy to," he replied, "as soon as you can find one family in the Bible I can use as an example." He was saying that perfect families, even in the Bible, simply don't exist. There are always those *people problems* that rise to break the mold. While the family at Bethany doesn't give us a perfect picture, it is probably about as close as one can come to finding a desirable role model.

Oh, I know what some will say: "But what about *pots and pans* Martha? You don't hold her up as a model to follow, do you?" As a matter of fact, I do, in all respects but one. Martha had a server's heart. Sitters aren't particularly comfortable with that attribute, so they have taken the occasion given by Jesus' rebuke in Luke 10:38-42 to heap scorn on that good and godly woman. Consequently, her entire character has been unfairly colored by a brush dipped in an incident. She was rebuked because she was serving when she should have been listening. Hers was a case of temporarily misplaced priorities, and Jesus chose to instruct her and us by pointing it out. It was not a matter of her being insensitive and inattentive to the Lord. Quite the contrary, Martha's servant heart caused her to attempt more than, in the Lord's view, the situation warranted. Servers often have that tendency—it's the way they're made. Let it be said in Martha's defense that it was she who welcomed Christ into their home (Lk. 10:38). It was Martha who first ran to meet the Lord following Lazarus' death (Jn. 11:20). It was she who expressed a knowledge of the Word and quality of faith that were equal to any projected in the Gospel records (Jn. 11:23-27). Listen to her: "Yea, Lord; I believe that thou art the Christ, the Son of God, who shall come into the world."

The big lesson coming to us from Martha and the home in Bethany is how to maintain our balance. Every quality needed in that quest is projected in John 12:1-11.

"*There they made him a supper, and Martha served. . . .*" Now unrebuked, Martha was serving. It was a time for service.

"*Then took Mary a pound of ointment of spikenard, very costly, and anointed the feet of Jesus, and wiped his feet with her hair. . . .*" Mary is seen lavishing her love upon her Lord in worship.

"*Many people of the Jews, therefore, knew that he was there; and they came, not for Jesus' sake only but that they might see Lazarus also, whom he had raised from the dead.*" Lazarus, who had been certified as dead, now sat entertaining guests in his home. He was irrefutable evidence of the divine power of Christ.

So we have:

Martha *working;*

Mary *worshiping;*

Lazarus *witnessing.* That, my friend, is the consummate pattern for a balanced life and home.

Martha Loved Him Too
Luke 10:38–42

But Martha was cumbered about much serving, and came to him, and said, Lord, dost thou not care that my sister hath left me to serve alone? Bid her, therefore, that she help me. And Jesus answered, and said unto her, Martha, Martha, thou art anxious and troubled about many things. But one thing is needful, and Mary hath chosen that good part, which shall not be taken away from her (vv. 40-42).

We've been too hard on Martha
   Because of that rebuff.
I think somehow we feel
   She didn't love her Lord enough.

No, quite to the contrary,
   Martha's love was such
That in her eagerness to serve,
   She tried to do too much.

For there's a time for serving,
   And there's a time for rest.
Everything in season;
   Choosing what is best.

That hour had its "good part"
   In sitting at His feet,
Taking in the blessed Word
   Which is our bread and meat.

Things must stay in balance,
   So let us pray from youth:
"God, give me Martha's diligence
And Mary's love for truth."

My Substitute

And when they were come to the place which is called Calvary, there they crucified him, and the malefactors, one on the right hand, and the other on the left (Lk. 23:33).

But he was wounded for our transgressions, he was bruised for our iniquities; the chastisement for our peace was upon him, and with his stripes we are healed. All we like sheep have gone astray; we have turned every one to his own way, and the LORD hath laid on him the iniquity of us all (Isa. 53:5-6).

From all black deeds of infamy
    The memory of man can frame,
One stands apart to numb the soul:
    Our God impaled in bloody shame.

Comes through the gloom a mystery,
    Now in His smitten flesh and bone
I view another fastened there,
    For in His face I see my own.

Then breaks a dawn of certainty,
    For deep in Christ's lone agony
There suffers 'neath my guilt in pain
    A Substitute who bleeds for me.

Mary at the Tomb
John 20:1-18

The first day of the week cometh Mary Magdalene early, when it was yet dark, unto the sepulcher, and seeth the stone taken away from the sepulcher (v. 1).

A Jewess came to a garden tomb
   On a chilly springtime day,
A mourner like those the world around
   Who pause at a grave to pray.
She'd walked as one whose scarlet life
   Had marked her path with scorn,
Until He came and made her pure
   As an infant summer's morn.
She loved and deigned to follow Him,
   This sinful one made clean.
For few have held affection true
   As did Mary Magdalene.
Lonely, she stood fast by the cross
   While strong men feared and fled.
With smitten spirit watched Him there
   As our stricken Savior bled.
Alone, she wept as she tread the path
   To the open sepulcher;
Wonderingly stooped down to look,
   When an angel beckoned her.
"Woman, why are you weeping?"
   Said a voice from the chamber dim.
"Because they've taken away my Lord,
   And I know not where they've laid Him."
Then came a word from a stranger's lips,
   His questions soft and clear:
"Whom do you seek in this place of death?
   Why stand you weeping here?"
"Oh, Sir, they've taken my Lord away
   And borne Him I know not where.

If you can tell of the place,
    I'll go to find Him there."
"Mary," spoke the living Christ,
    "Rabboni," her reply.
Her Master lives! Exultant praise
    Now gilds the morning sky.
A Jewess rushed from a garden tomb
    To raise a triumphant chord,
A song of hope for every man:
    "I've seen the risen Lord!"

GARDENS

And they heard the voice of the LORD God walking in the garden in the cool of the day . . . (Gen. 3:8).

Man started out in a garden, working with his hands in a little corner of God's creation. Until a generation or so ago, gardens were part of the experience of most people growing up in this country. That isn't true any longer, and I don't think we're better off for it. There's a great deal to be learned in a garden. For example, you learn about creation and how God does things. You also learn a lot about work and practice getting things done on time.

Whether you ever hear them use the term or not, *discipline* is the big word with good gardeners—Adam and Eve, you'll remember, had some trouble with that concept. Old-timers believed big gardens worked wonders in small boys who needed to be taught the right things—things like watching where you step, what not to pull up, or what to cut down. Some young fellows take to these lessons more readily than others.

Faces on the Garden Path

My father subscribed to the old-timers' credo that large gardens grew good boys. He had twin problems to reckon with: How to put enough food on the table in those Great Depression years; and keeping three active boys occupied during long summer days—idle hands are a parent's grief. We would stand before him in the morning while he assigned our "chores" for the day. Then it was off to work for him, and off to the garden for us. Walter was the eldest. Heavy jobs like cultivating fell to him. Ken was younger, so he didn't have a lot to do—mostly piddle and stay out of the way. I was the middle boy, and, as I remember things, I did an inordinate amount of weeding.

Did you ever weed carrots? If the weeds are thick, you can't see them—that is, until you pull one up—thin orange shafts. Carrots don't seem to do well when you stick them back in the ground.

I preferred to bury the evidence completely. A curious thing about pulling weeds—non-weeders may not grasp this—is as the day wears on the rows seem to get longer and longer. I don't know that I ever found the end of one. And it gets hot, maybe because weeders stay so close to the ground.

By midmorning I would begin seeing apparitions coming down the garden path. They all wore the bright face of temptation, and each offered a sound reason why I should leave the garden: "Go for water"; "Don't stay out here till you make yourself sick"; "They need a shortstop over at the ball field." So, armed with good reasons and better intentions, I spent many afternoons recovering by chasing balls and boys across vacant lots.

Trouble was, a fellow always had to come home. That's especially problematic for people with bad timing who arrive just after dad gets in from work. Waiting for that last turn at bat had a way of placing me in that position. But, not to worry, my carefully prepared *reasons* would stand up before the highest courts in the land. The only hitch was, they never did—they were seldom even offered.

The interrogation went something like this.

Father: "Where have you been?"

Son: "Playing ball."

Father: "Did you finish your chores?"

Son: "No, but I'll do it tomorrow."

Father: "Didn't I tell you I wanted this finished today?"

Son: "Yes, sir."

Father: "Did you understand me?"

Son: "Yes, sir."

Father: "Then why didn't you do it?"

It was at precisely this point that my carefully accumulated *reasons* were supposed to leap in, quell any further questions, and send us off to supper with a warm feeling of father-son camaraderie. Unfortunately, at this juncture my memory would go stone cold, and I would become a functional mute. Anyway, those *reasons* seemed to lose their pungency at about this time.

I took some trips to the woodshed over those encounters. We didn't even have a woodshed, but boys my age didn't need a mental reconstruction of that artifact of ancient history to get the picture. All of us knew, too well, what it meant to have the opportunity to dance in the woodshed.

Big gardens do grow good boys—at least boys—at least boys who know better.

My father's questions taught me things about my relationship to God which will provide, I think, the basis for evaluating our service at the Judgment Seat of Christ. "Did you hear and believe My Word? Did you do it? If not, why not?"

Funny thing about that old garden, one of the most solemn vows of my boyhood (and boys tend to make a lot of solemn vows) was, once liberated, never to work in a garden again. Never! I thought about that on a return trip back to Virginia from Michigan some years ago. "Mom," I said, "do you have a big box I could use?" "Sure, out back," she replied. "Then would you mind if I used it to get some dirt from the garden to take home with me? I think it will be just the thing to use in my garden to soften up the radish patch."

Growing Jonah's Gourd

But God appointed a worm when dawn came the next day, and it attacked the plant and it withered. And it came about when the sun came up that God appointed a scorching east wind, and the sun beat down . . . (Jon. 4:7–8 N.A.S.B.).

Support arrangements with our first church were simple: $45.00 a week and members filled the freezer with meat in the fall. Granted, a dollar rolled a bit farther then than now; still, keeping the larder full called for some applied ingenuity.

As a man who had done his time in the garden, and with vows I would never do it again reluctantly abandoned, I decided a vegetable garden would plug some noticeable holes in the family budget. The Lord would, I was sure, honor our efforts with an abundant yield;

and it would also be a good testimony to members of the community, some of whom were somewhat skeptical about a preacher's commitment to manual labor.

Tom, our oldest boy, and I surveyed a neatly plowed, raked, rowed, and planted garden plot. "There's only one thing left to do now," I said with unrestrained satisfaction, "we'll have prayer and ask the Lord to give us a good harvest." Tom would profit, I thought, from watching the garden grow and witnessing answered prayer in action.

We were dismayed to discover, however, that current plans for our part of the world called for a dry spring. Under such conditions our well lacked the capacity for washing and watering at the same time, so watching the garden dry up and blow away became a dismal daily occupation. A symbolic chasm in the catastrophe opened as I stood looking into a yawning crack in the parched soil. An emaciated bean sprout, struggling to reach ground level, was being assaulted by a band of ravenous insects. Needless to say, the bean was losing the battle.

Jonah, I lamented, had done better with his gourd. At least it had had enough early growth to shed a little shade before it died. Jonah and I did have a common complaint however. Dead gourds and dead beans add up to the same result: expired hopes.

As things turned out, I suspect for both Jonah and yours truly, the Lord's answer provided much more fruit than that garden could have produced in a lifetime. For He did answer our prayer, and in wonderfully explicit ways. It was just that His arrangement was somewhat different from what I had envisioned.

Throughout the summer we would discover bags of beans, greens, cucumbers, potatoes, and plump tomatoes on our front porch. Unlike my hilltop tract, close-to-the-creek gardens were producing bumper crops, and we were joyfully sharing the bounty. The Lord had planned it this way, and, once again, His way proved to be far better than our way. When I finally realized what was going on, I reaped some mental fruit to savor over the years. As a young preacher ministered the Word to his people, they ministered to him and his family. In the process, each had the satisfaction of doing what the Lord had prepared them to do best. We were all enriched by the experience.

Grandsons and Gardens

Garden lessons aren't the exclusive right of the young. Elders can as quickly garner fresh insights from little gardeners who are companions in toil. I learned something from a five-year-old grandson on a day not unlike some I spent in my father's vegetable park. Hot and sultry was the forecast, and the day delivered on that promise.

When Brent came to spend a day with us, he found me in our little garden tending weeds. "What are you doing, papaw?" he asked.

"I'm working to get rid of some of these old weeds," I said, exhibiting my boyhood disgust for things too dumb to know their proper place.

"Can I help?" he inquired with boyish enthusiasm.

"You sure can," I answered, directing him to a hoe I had laid at a corner of the lot. That was a mistake. My grandson didn't know crabgrass from cucumbers, and his gusto in swinging his implement of destruction put some fine plants in serious jeopardy. Soon sweat was running from his tightly curled hair and streaking his forehead.

I could see grandma looking out from the kitchen window occasionally, keeping an eye on proceedings out back. After a while, she came through the door carrying two glasses of tea for the perspiring farmhands. She brought some advice along with the cool liquid. "It's awfully hot out here for a boy to be working as hard as you seem to be. You'd better sit in the shade and cool off while papaw finishes his job." Brent drew himself up to a ramrod straight position and looked his grandmother in the eye.

"It's all right grandma. Whatever papaw says to do is OK with me!" What a grandson—brilliant boy—I thought. The greatest thing in his life at that moment was serving his papaw. We were in touch and in tune. It was a wonderful moment.

Later, when I ran over it in my mind, I was impressed with just how good it would be if we all reflected his exuberance and unqualified commitment in our service for the Lord. We would be on line, front and center, awaiting His orders; doing His will and exhibiting a joy-laden eagerness which says for all to hear: "Whatever my Lord says to do is OK with me!" Such an attitude could just be the seed plot for a revival—could it not?

Kneeling in the Garden

Jim was raised far off the beaten track in rural Virginia. I first met him when I became his pastor back in the early 50s. He was a simple, steadfast Christian, the kind of person God uses to mark your own life in significant ways. He got off to a bad start as a motherless, unschooled boy living with a family which had little regard for God and none at all for formal training. Consequently, Jim learned early about sawmilling, hunting, and drinking. By the time he was a teenager, moonshine had gotten the best of him. He was living a wrenchingly deplorable life. Jim desperately needed help. It came by way of a memory. You see, Jim's mother had lived for a few brief years after he had come into the world. Those precious days under her love and care would provide memories that would bring him to Christ.

Like all women of the community, Jim's mother worked a patch of land set aside for growing the vegetables families ate in summer and put up in cans to see them through the winter months. You could see them early in the mornings in their poke bonnets bending over long green rows intently pulling beans or peas from reluctant vines. The path to the spring ran through their garden, so early each day, with little Jim behind and bucket in hand, she would travel the path to dip up their water supply for the day. A gnarled fruit tree stood beside the path at the edge of the garden. On summer days, when they reached the tree, Jim's mother would stop, put down her bucket, and kneel with him at her side. There she would pray for Jim, for God to save him and make him a good boy. She went home to Heaven when he was four or five. He lost her, but never the memory. It would burn in his befuddled mind as he later tried to sort things out and make sense of life. How he yearned to find what she had shown him on those bright mornings in the garden.

Jim decided to go looking for it. The white clapboard-sided church on the hill would be the place to start, he reckoned. So he showed up one Sunday morning, listened, and God answered his mother's prayer—Jim was saved.

Jim

Jim was a man of the country—
　　Tall and tempered lean.
He'd seen the rough of rural ways
　　When the winter's winds blew mean.

Jim had a Christian mother,
　　She loved her scrawny boy
And sang him songs of Jesus' love,
　　Of Heaven, peace, and joy.

At morning's light he'd go with her
　　Down a winding garden way
To lift a bucket from the spring
　　For the needs of another day.

Before they reached the house again
　　They'd stop by a gnarled fruit tree.
She'd kneel with him to greet the day
　　With a prayer for her Jimmie Lee.

Then came a raw December morn
　　When he walked the path alone.
His mother's death and the winter's chill
　　Left him cold as her gray gravestone.

Without a mother's hand and prayers
　　The lad was easy prey
For the foul-mouthed, drunken ne'er-do-wells
　　Who walked in the Devil's way.

Young Jim would come to manhood
　　A sad-faced sight to see,
Far from the eager, bright-eycd boy
　　Who'd bowed at his mother's knee.

He'd traded school to spend his days
　　In the dust of an old sawmill.
Come night, he'd drink till the stupor came
　　Near a wooded mountain still.

But when Jim fell on his rumpled bed
　　To toss through a fitful night,
He'd see a tree, and a little boy,
　　And a morning sun full bright.

Again he'd hear his mother pray
　　For God to save her Jim,
Keep her son in the narrow way
　　To live and honor Him.

Years would steal some memories
　　From the mind of Jimmie Lee,
But ne'er the sight of a gnarled fruit tree
　　And a boy at his mother's knee.

One Sunday morn, when the sun shone bright
　　On a clapboard country church,
Jim walked in and took a seat—
　　He'd come there on a search.

To seek out what his mother'd had
　　In those days so long ago;
To make his peace with God above,
　　And be clean as the driven snow.

A sleepy crowd came quick awake
    At the sight of Jimmie Lee.
The preacher swung the gospel sword,
    It fell to cut him free.

While they all sang, young Jim stepped out
    To make his break with sin;
To bend the knee by an old church pew
    And ask the Savior in.

It's "Old Jim" now, and talk he will
    Of those days by an old fruit tree,
But better still of a day to come
    When he'll share her victory!

Jim shares his mother's victory today. A few years after this poem was written we gathered at the church cemetery to remember Jim, his mother, and the garden path that was his way to glory.

Grandchildren

Some people have little time for those who make even passing reference to their grandchildren. I place these detractors into two general categories: 1. They don't have grandkids themselves. 2. They are probably not the kind of people grandchildren would want to spend much time around anyway. It makes one wonder what these impatient folk do when they encounter children who are bursting to tell wonderful tales about their grandparents.

I was preaching at a church in Virginia not long ago. The evening service had concluded, and I had slipped into the vestibule to greet the people as they were leaving. A boy, I judged to be eight or nine, was the first parishioner to exit. It was immediately obvious that he was in deep distress and could afford no delays in getting to the men's room. He threw up a hand as he passed, made a quick turn to the right, sped through double glass doors, and made a charge up the stairs. Halfway up he stopped, whirled on his heel, ran back down, pushed the door open a bit, and stuck his head out. "Do you know Preacher Ernest Slaughter?" he asked.

"Yes, I do," I replied.

With a look that said it all, he called back, "He's my grandpa!" Without another word, he returned to the business at hand.

I don't know much about how "Preacher Ernest Slaughter" does as a pulpiteer, but I know he's marking at least one proud grandson for God.

For my part, I want my grandchildren to think I'm the greatest grandpa who ever pulled on a pair of socks. It's working pretty well to this point. We attend the same church as our son and daughter-in-law, which serves two central purposes. Our pastor feeds us excellent messages from God's Word, and we also have a weekly chance to check in with two of our grandsons.

I was passing through the Sunday School department where Brent, three at the time, attended class. It was between services, and he and several of his friends were sitting around a table talking over significant matters. He stopped me with a question: "Who will be in the nursery today?"

"I'll see," I said, leafing through the bulletin. Finding the name he wanted, I filled him in and resumed my journey. As I departed, his voice drifted over my shoulder.

"You see what I told you," he said triumphantly. "My papaw knows just about everything there is to know about anything!"

His younger brother Josh summed things up for both of us the other day as I was taking him home after a full day at our house. We had done the whole routine, capped off by enjoying fine cuisine at McDonald's and the inevitable romp in the playground. Getting him off the slide always takes some serious negotiation. Our usual compromise is ice cream—he's a pushover for a strawberry sundae. Strapped securely in the front seat of the car as we headed home (at three he can't see over the dashboard), he looked up and said exactly what his granddad had been thinking: "You know, papaw, the day just kinda got away from us, didn't it?" It sure did, Josh. It sure did.

He had been in this world just 20 months when he taught me some things about myself and gave me a sound lesson to pass on to other granddads. Josh had learned to somersault, so when he and his mom walked into the house he immediately put on an exhibition of his just-found physical prowess. Over and over he tumbled, clear across the living room floor. "Did you see that! Did you see that!" I exclaimed. This was, to my strictly unprejudiced eye, perhaps the greatest display of physical dexterity ever demonstrated by a 20-month old in the entire history of humanity. He was smug; his mother was pleased as punch; grandma and I were impressed.

I was so impressed, I decided I'd do one for him. It was a big mistake. Some time had passed since I had done one of those things, and I quickly learned that parts of my body just don't work like they once did. As the room careened about my head at dizzying angles and my body rigidly descended, I was entertaining thoughts from childhood about how the leaning tower of Pisa would look when it finally crashed to the ground.

Maxine gave the report. "When you hit the floor," she giggled— enjoying it a bit too much to suit me—"the piano leaped up and hovered for awhile before it came back down again."

They got a laugh; I got a lesson. Pay attention grandpas, and you can learn one too.

The Last Somersault

I did a somersault today,
Not likely I'll do more.
Vertebrae all snapped and cracked
As body shook the floor.
If asked to duplicate the feat
By president or king,
My answer will be resolute:
"I'll venture no such thing!"
But it was grandson Joshua I'd

Set out to impress,
So papaw hurled his torso forth
In obvious distress.
He thought it entertaining,
And flashed a crooked grin.
A look to last a lifetime—
I'll not somersault again.

A quietly disconcerting thing about being, as I am, papaw is the thought that mine is not a permanent distinction. Oh, I'll always be their grandfather, no matter how many grandkids our children grace us with. But that's just the point: eventually papaws turn into grandfathers. It just goes along with growing up. I'm not there yet, but I just suspect graduating to grandfather is going to take a lot of fun out of the position. I don't know if I'll enjoy being *grandfather-proud* of grown grandkids quite as much as I do being *papaw-patsie* to the little ones. Of course, rational men know that each step forward produces satisfaction commensurate with your progress. And, as a self-regarded rational man, I realize that it is quite likely I will someday look back and see how foolish I was to wonder about it all. For now, though, I must confess to these feelings:

On Being Papaw

Funny how these grandkids
Run right in and grab your heart.
Know just how to do it.
They really are quite smart.

It's "Papaw, look," or "Papaw,
Come," or "Papaw, what'd ya bring?"
That kind of popularity's a rare
And precious thing.

So play hard and enjoy it.
Go at it tooth and tong.
Just think of this old-timer:
You can't stay papaw long.

Too soon I'll turn to Grandfather,
Enrobed in dignity.
But I confess that prospect
Holds scant appeal for me.

I'll have to sit with grown-up folk,
And talk of grown-up ways.
No wonder grandpas sleep a lot.
They dream of better days.

See, grandkids grant us one last chance
To live life's childhood stage.
Devoid of caustic repartee:
"Why don't you act your age!"

If ever I could keep one thing
From all life's favored joys,
I might choose staying papaw—
On the floor among the toys.

First Words

Being there when a baby utters first words is a thrilling experience (though we sometimes wonder why when besieged by torrents of talk in later months and years). Grandmas and grandpas feel especially proud when they are favored with a child's initial discourse.

We were standing before the old Ingram school clock hanging over our mantel. Grandma was holding Brent up so he could watch the big pendulum follow its lazy back-and-forth track. He was mesmerized by the movement.

Suddenly, he imitated the sound. "Tick-tock," he said. His look told us the story: He had entered the world of the verbally proficient, and he was happy to have arrived.

"Tick-tock," he said
   To our surprise,
A guileless twinkle
   In his eyes.
Mother gasped,
   And I said, "Oh!"
His little face
   Took on a glow.
Now we were sure
   The world took note
And registered
   His famous quote.
So we were smug
   At what was done
By our articulate
   Grandson.

Reaching Fifty

Live joyfully with the wife whom thou lovest all the days of the life of thy vanity, which he hath given thee under the sun, all the days of thy vanity; for that is thy portion in this life... (Eccl. 9:9).

Our home has always been a place where we have done a great deal of laughing. Now, when the children are in for the holidays, evenings are punctuated by mirthful remembrances of how things used to be when they were growing up. Often, of course, mom and dad are the objects of their hilarity. Maxine had the stage all to herself when I read this poem, written to help her remember birthday number fifty.

You may think it nifty
To have arrived at fifty,
While making people wonder
If you are not much younger.
So if you wish to whittle
Your age down just a little,
With me will be just fine
If you stay forty-nine.
And if I'm asked to say
How old you are today,
I'll deftly wink an eye;
I'll play it coy and sly.
And say, "It's not her age
That should your mind engage,
From blossom full mature
Shines floral beauty pure.
Only fruit that's ripe and mellow
Can please a hungry fellow.
And, yes, a touch of roundness
Speaks clear of robust soundness.
The velvet in her eyes
Shows one who's truly wise
To our thoughts and ways and needs,

To our striving and our deeds.
Now when they flay and scold me,
On her bosom soft she'll hold me.
Friend, she makes it all seem better,
And, you know, I love to let her."
So the years did not diminish,
They have just improved your finish!

The Peaks

Virginia is a place of compelling beauty. One of our favorite spots on the Blue Ridge Parkway is the Peaks of Otter. In fall, when the leaves are sun-splashed in variegated glory against the mountains, or in spring as the rhododendron comes into full flower, it's difficult to imagine a more beautiful setting anywhere on earth. For 35 years we've gone there for rest and relaxation. On early outings, when the children were small, we climbed Sharptop, a mountain that tested limb and lung. More recently, just the two of us go there to eat at the lodge and stroll by the lake. We also do a lot of reminiscing.

It's quiet up here in these mountains—
   good for thinking, or just walking hand-in-hand.
Today the rain makes dimples on the lake,
    while apples on a twisted tree show bright red
      in protest of the sullen skies.
The mountain is hiding her head beneath a thick cloud.
Perhaps she's tired of looking down at all the people
   looking up at her.
She's getting older, but she wears it well.
And we understand, for we are older too.
We first saw her thirty years ago.
Since then, she's kept an eye on us,
   and we on her.
I can't count all the times we've brought our children here
   to scamper to the top,
     look her over,
       then try to find our house hidden off somewhere
       among the lush green valleys.
We don't have much scamper left in us now.
The kids are gone, except one, and he fancies himself
   too old to come along.

So, most times, we come by ourselves to share a tranquil meal,
    look out across the lake,
        and talk.
Some, I guess, would think it rather sad to see us here this way,
    without them.
It isn't.
Because we know where they all are—
    safe and well.
And, anyway, we can see their forms all over the mountain—
    shining little faces once again.
Why, we can almost hear them squealing their pleasure
    back and forth as they run the footbridges,
        or glimpse a fleeing deer.
No, we don't mourn the passing of our youth;
    things are just fine now.
We have these memories, and time for ourselves.
Just us,
    the way we started out so very long ago.
To me, you'll always be the auburn-haired girl
    in the picture,
        with this old mountain standing patiently behind to frame
            your lovely face.
So we'll keep coming,
    when I'm tired from the road
        and you of the house.
We'll savor this place they call the Peaks,
    sit together,
        and say how good it is to be up here once again.

Ottervue

Ottervue was six hundred acres of lush Virginia landscape surrounding a stately country house and outbuildings. The farm was perpetually on loan to us by gracious friends. We tramped the woods, watched fat tadpoles dart about the pond, ran the back roads, and lunched by an old sawmill. Nothing on earth, it seemed to us, quite matched the view there as the sun withdrew slowly beyond the blue mountains and darkness began to embrace the red hills and rustic structures. Such was our Ottervue. Where is yours?

> God has His best upon this sphere
> Of plan, of place, and time,
> To pass our days, to dream our dreams,
> And find His rest sublime.
>
> To love this land, to nourish it,
> To work the rich red soil,
> Will bring full measure from the earth
> To recompense our toil.
>
> The sun sprinkled a rushing stream
> Then washed these fields today,
> Where brown-flecked fawns stood quietly
> While calves were at their play.
>
> We sit beneath these great green trees
> Possessed by mountain's hue.
> This is God's best for you and me—
> Our place, our Ottervue.

Masada and Calvary

Israel has two dominating symbols. In eloquent silence they stand for all the world to see; they speak for all the world to hear. Masada memorializes a national tragedy: the fall of Jerusalem in 70 A.D. On its summit, high above the Judean wilderness, Jewish survivors of the Roman holocaust took their own lives rather than submit to tyrants. The event was the emotional watermark from which the tide of the dispersion swept Jewry into two thousand years of wandering and, too often, suffering. Today, Jews go there to remember their Masadas, national and personal, and resolutely intone words that have become the watchword of the modern state of Israel, "Masada shall not fall again."

In a quiet little garden, just outside the walls of Old Jerusalem, is an open doorway. Beyond the threshold is an ancient tomb—the tomb is empty. From that garden one can look up to the crest of a small hill, a promontory believed by many to be Mount Calvary, the site of Jesus' crucifixion. Whether this is the actual place or not matters little. The salient point is that there was a Calvary, and there is an empty tomb! Together they echo the reality of a living, conquering Savior who suffered once that there need never be another sacrificial altar. Through His death, all men, Jew and Gentile alike, have the opportunity to receive eternal life and liberation from sin, death, and hell.

Will Masada's trauma be relived? No, thank God, because, as incomprehensible as it may seem at the moment, Masada and Calvary stand in juxtaposition. Israel will one day come to her Armageddon, but out of that consummating confrontation her reconciling Messiah will be revealed. Then the nation will join in a triumphal procession toward a higher summit.

And so all Israel shall be saved; as it is written, There shall come out of Zion the Deliverer, and shall turn away ungodliness from Jacob; For this is my covenant unto them, when I shall take away their sins (Rom. 11:26–27).

Masada—Never Again!

Rome hailed it as a monument
    to death,
        a sullen token of futility,
That subject peoples all might
    stare and say,
        "Rome is our master;
           Empire is supreme."

E'en the name of that foreboding
    place,
        standing stark hard by
           the sterile sea,
MASADA conjures darkened memories
    of those who stood to fight,
        then stayed to die.
"Jews must learn," a laurel-crowned
    Caesar said,
        "to bow the knee beneath
           their sovereign's hand.
They have no power to stay the
    legions' might.
        Pitiful people,
           Kneel or feed the sword."
But tyrants often do more
    than they know,
        For from their follies
           symbols tend to rise,
Then stand like specters over
    future days, and whisper,
        as they pass their fitful nights,
        a people's firm resolve:
MASADA—Never again!

Old Jews slowly mount that
    summit now,
        remembering Masadas they
        once knew.
They contemplate grim scenes
    from other days,
        of friends cut off before
        their days were full.
And turning faces to Judean skies,
    they whisper low:
MASADA—Never Again!

Sturdy sabras line the plateaued
    brow.
Olive garbed, they've come
    to raise the word.
Theirs to face the thrust
    of metaled death;
        theirs to say for all the world
        to hear:
MASADA—Never Again!

Children swing along the winding
    path,
        sharing strains of Israel's
        joy and hope.
Their melodies invade the winds,
    and mount to trumpet
        Jewry's fondest dream:
        to dwell in peace upon
        old Zion's hills,
            and live the dream:
MASADA—Never Again!

Gentiles gather there to scan
   the view,
      their spirits foreign to
         the Caesar's kin,
To learn of struggle, sacrifice,
   and death,
      of Jews whose will could not
         be overcome,
Who deemed to die in their own land
   far better choice
      than life in captive's cell.
Then Jew and Gentile friend
   stand side by side
      to clasp the hand
         and join the solemn pledge:
MASADA—Never Again!

CALVARY—Never Again!

To Pilate it was minor compromise,
  one small concession made to serve an end.
That Roman guard might know
  a peaceful night
    devoid of strident cries
    and milling throng.

Within the High Priest's court
  a sigh was raised.
The matter was resolved,
  the issue done.
This One who raised the rabble's
  hope was dead,
    and with Him rested a
      delusive dream of being
        God and man, Messiah-King.

Time, they thought, would serve
  to do its work,
    and full unmask the Dreamer's
    manic claim.
Theirs but to watch and wait
  at chamber side.

Yet quite beyond their view
  another stood
    to savor memories of
    the lash and tree.
For Lucifer it was triumph
  supreme.
He'd met his Maker's Christ
  and laid Him low.
No matter that the Nazarene
  approached His cross
    with confidence
      and word He'd rise again.

Death and quiet held sway
    in the tomb,
        and Satan saw himself
            as Sovereign Star.

But word rang clear in Heaven·
    "All is well!"
For from a brooding hill
    where once He hung
        echoed still
            His message true:
                "It is finished!"
And that transaction, thus complete,
    would shine emblazoned by
        confirming word:
            "He is not here,
                but is risen
                    as He said."
Now over all peals one resounding
    strain:
CALVARY—Never Again!

Believing Jews approach
    that withered hill,
        and contemplate how truly
            it could be
                that God, as man, could come
                and suffer there
                    to once-for-all
                        relieve sin's burden sore.

Then lifting thankful voices
    join the heavenly song:
CALVARY—Never Again!

Gentiles wonder at the herald's word,
   how on a wooden cross
     He'd choose to die.
And how believing on His finished work
   they, too, could stand at
     His once-riven side.

With hearts and voices clear they
   hymn the phrase:
CALVARY—Never Again!

So man and seraphim survey the scene;
   the study of the ages, all agree.
Out of death came life,
   and peace sublime from cruelest
     agony.
No more would ever an altar
   need be raised
     where sacrifice would suffer,
       bleed, and die.
It was enough for Him to taste our death
   that we might rise with Him to say:
CALVARY—Never Again!

Jerusalem

Jerusalem holds the heart of Jewry in ways impossible to comprehend unless one understands that God has implanted a surpassing love for the place in the anatomy of the Jew. This phenomenon is shared in measure by Christians who find a magnetic attachment to the city which beckons them to return again and again. And why not? The Holy City will one day soon receive our triumphant Lord as He returns to this planet in power and glory. And from Jerusalem He will establish a thousand-year reign in which His righteousness and knowledge will cover the earth as the waters fill the seas. Our attachment then will be not to a place, wonderful as it may be, but to One who fills our hearts and the universe.

And his feet shall stand in that day upon the Mount of Olives, which is before Jerusalem on the east . . . And the LORD shall be king over all the earth (Zech. 14:4, 9).

> Of all the regal cities fair
>   The planet can display,
> None will ever yet compare
>   With that one far away.
> A solitary maiden there
>   Upon the sun-drenched hills,
> Glistening domes and treasures rare
>   The voyager's vision fills.
> From all the centuries of old
>   Dust-laden men have trod
> To wrest her from another's hold
>   And make her serve their god.
> But one by one they're turned aside
>   That all men might confess:
> What Gentile lords have been denied,
>   Jehovah will possess.

The Wailing Wall

See the Hebrew standing there
　　Before the ancient stones.
He lifts his voice o'er downcast eyes
　　In soft but plaintive tones.
He comes here to remember;
　　He comes here to forget;
To mourn departed glories,
　　And dream what might be yet.
From memory, sunken faces
　　File by in gaunt parade.
Now comes the haughty Sabra
　　Resolute and unafraid.
Symbol to the scattered tribes,
　　Great sentinel of the years,
Emblem of all Jewry,
　　Receptacle of tears.
Mute witness to her sufferings
　　And yearnings for release,
Give substance to the promise
　　Of Israel's coming peace.

The Holy City

Seat of David's hallowed throne,
   Salem, City of Peace.
Plagued of death by sword and stone
   Until all wars shall cease.
Long thy sons have wandered far
   The captive's chain to bear.
Now, back home, the Royal Star
   They look with pride to wear.
The prophets warn of coming strife
   To smite the remnant there,
But over this shine words of life
   Which vanquish brooding care.
For David's Greater Son, you see,
   Will save and rule the nation.
The Holy City then shall be
   The center of creation.

The Jew

Our fascination with the miracle of the rebirth of Israel has diminished greatly over the forty years of her modern existence. Today, as the world gangs up on Israel with renewed ferocity, Christians should be reminded that only God's providence could transform the beleaguered "Wandering Jew" into the modern Israeli; and that the Jewish presence in the Middle East portends all God has promised to accomplish in the last days.

We well recall the wandering Jew
   Bowed low and slow of gait,
Who crept the ghettos, wore the patch,
   Absorbed the scorn and hate.

He sold us matches, bought our rags,
   Sewed clothes, and fixed the shoes.
But seldom would we fraternize,
   Strange ones, we thought, those Jews.

It seemed he never quite belonged;
   His gaze was fixed afar.
It was as though he searched the skies
   To find some rising star.

One day he left, quite suddenly,
   That earnest son of Shem,
"I'm going home; I've found my star:
   Beloved Jerusalem!"

He's down on Ben Yehuda Street,
   Erect and bronzed and trim.
Now we stand by in silent awe
   To hear and learn from him.

God's Way

I say, then, Have they stumbled that they should fall? God forbid; but rather through their fall salvation is come unto the Gentiles, to provoke them to jealousy . . . For the gifts and the calling of God are without repentance (Rom. 11:11, 29).

Persistent anti-Semitism has demonstrated the depths of mankind's depravity over the centuries. Time and again, Jewry has been inundated by her own blood as wave after wave of vehement hostility has swept over the sons and daughters of Abraham. But God warns in His Word that correcting these people is not a prerogative left with men. The Lord alone can employ chastisement in His plan to ultimately bring the Jewish people to Himself.

> Lay not a hand on the sons of His choosing,
>   Bowed by oppression, beset with despair.
> Yours but to comfort and pray for His people;
>   Yours but to tell them of Christ's loving care.
>
> Chastisement comes from the hand of the Father.
>   His, only His, to bring down the rod.
> Then, when the lesson is learned in repentance,
>   Eyes turn with hearts toward Israel's God.
>
> Yours then and mine to show our allegiance—
>   Love for Messiah and His kinsmen too,
> Thus God speaks softly to Abraham's children,
>   Breathing His heart-love through those born anew.

Born a Jew

"Was born a Jew, I'll die a Jew!"
And so you will, my friend.
For Abram's sons are bound to him
By cords which none can rend.

But being of his flesh and blood,
Thus born of high degree,
Cannot assure eternal life—
From sin forever free.

Of Spirit's seed each one must come
To be of royal birth.
And to this end Messiah came
To do His work on earth.

It's by His finished sacrifice,
Through faith in God's I AM,
That true-born sons of Abraham
Are worthy in the Lamb.

To the Jew, Too!

Long and heated discussions have waged on the subject of our witness to Jewish people. "It must be to the Jew first," some will argue. In light of the indifference among many believers toward their responsibility to share Christ with Jewish people, however, a more appropriate question would seem to be, "Is the Jew being given equal time? Do we really believe that the gospel is to the Jew, too?"

For there is no difference between the Jew and the Greek; for the same Lord over all is rich unto all that call upon him. For whosoever shall call upon the name of the Lord shall be saved (Rom. 10:12–13).

> Could I soar to seize the world
>   and hold its title clear,
> I'd give it all to share the Christ
>   with those our Lord holds dear.
> Sons of Jacob, loved of God,
>   will one day know their King.
> Those who tell this word today
>   can do no better thing.

Invaders

Long they looked with hungry eyes
    At Canaan's storied land.
Stealthily conspired to come
    And take the deed in hand.

Columned armies, turbaned hosts,
    Dark Bedouin marauder,
Swept with fury o'er the hills
    To seize Jehovah's daughter.

With dented shield and blunted sword
    They all would trudge away,
And learn that only Jacob's sons
    Could enter there to stay.

Armageddon

When all our friends deserted,
  While vicious foes assailed,
We looked for consolation,
  But every means had failed.

Our eyes now search the heavens,
  Red-rimmed with bitter shame,
At our long-time refusal
  To call Messiah's name.

Then rend these war-soiled garments,
  Our cry before Him rings:
"Come Savior-Christ, deliver!"
  Behold, the KING OF KINGS.

The Six Day War
June, 1967

Little David stood one day
  Before a glowering foe.
Trembling brothers watched from far
  To see him come to woe.
Sang his sling with high-pitched note
  As stone launched from its seat.
Soon a quivering despot's form
  Lay at the stripling's feet.

Little Israel stood one day
  Before an enemy,
Who boasted loud and promised all
  He'd drive her to the sea.
Midst turbine's whine and surging tanks,
  With charging infantry,
David's sons brought down their foe
  And rewrote history.

Jehovah Answers
Ezekiel 38, 39

"I will call for a sword," Jehovah has said,
And leave the Red hordes to number their dead.
To strike with a shaking, the flood and great hail,
My spear gleaming lightning to pierce through their mail.
Dread silence will reign on the face of the land,
All ears fallen deaf to the sound of command.
Now frozen in death hands that wielded the sword,
Brought low in the end by the voice of the Lord.
So birds wing their way where once raged the strife,
To light midst the shambles, bereft of all life.
Behold, it is done, and let it be known,
The arm of Jehovah was bared for His own.

Gideon's Band

Stand in your places
 With lamps held alighted.
Wait for the trumpet
 To call to the fray.
Stand tall and strong
 In the strength of Jehovah.
For His three hundred
 Will triumph today!

The Chosen People
Numbers 24

E'en from the tongues and lives
   Of men unwilling,
God moves in silent majesty
   His ancient will fulfilling.

While hireling Balaam plies his mind
   A blighting curse to raise,
An unseen hand molds sneering lips
   To instruments of praise.

And so it is with Abram's sons
   Through all successive years,
Wild arrogance from wanton men
   And flowing Jewish tears.

Thus man would strip the Hebrews
   Of their promises foretold
And give them only refuse while
   The Gentiles gather gold.

But wonder of the ages,
   Two miracles resound:
The sons of Jacob are preserved;
   They seek their ancient ground!

The unseen hand now moves again
   And Jews are homeward driven
To that promised land of Isaac
   By God forever given.

Still, while invective curses come
   From East, and South, and North,
They gather at the Wailing Wall
   To plead His coming forth.

And though her trouble lies ahead
   In sorest tribulation,
He soon will come and reign supreme
   O'er His beloved nation.

STONEWALL AND JASPER

There are no barriers too formidable for the grace of God to remove, no walls grace cannot scale. History often demonstrates this in ways and circumstances which seem most improbable to human observers. A prime illustration was demonstrated in the lives of John Jasper and Thomas Jonathan "Stonewall" Jackson. The time of their lives was America's most traumatic, the Civil War. Jasper and Jackson lived on opposite sides of the largest obstacles of the times. The blue/gray barrier divided the country, the black/white issue its people.

The next two pieces tell once again the age-old story of the efficiency of God's grace in penetrating whatever obstacles man erects in order to do His eternal work in human hearts and lives.

Go Tell 'em, John!

Black wasn't beautiful down in Fluvanna County, Virginia, in 1812. As Tina Jasper looked into the face of her newborn son—child number 24—the Peachey family up in the "great house" was appreciative that they could register their ownership of another body and look to the day when he could provide a strong back and two hands to work the fields of their sprawling plantation.

Philip, the child's father, had been a minister of sorts, preaching, as slaves were permitted, at funeral services for his fellow servants. He died a few months before the child was born.

Prospects were not good for John Jasper, but one thing he did have working for him: His mother was a godly, praying woman, and claiming this boy for God would become a central mission in her life.

As a lad John was bounced about, serving first as a cartboy. When old enough to become a field hand, he was frequently shifted from one part of the estate to another. He did some time in the coal pits at Chesterfield and was shuttled elsewhere before finally being hired out to Samuel Hargrove, who later purchased him outright. Hargrove took John to Richmond.

By the time he settled in Richmond as a gangling 22-year-old, Jasper carried an acute awareness of the hopeless frustration and bitterness slavery was so adept at delivering. His deepest wound had been inflicted after he had fallen in love with Elvie Weeden, who served on another plantation.

The night of their marriage happened to coincide with an attempted mass escape by slaves from the Peachey estate. Armed men, immediately dispatched to retrieve the runaways, found John and Elvie alone in their honeymoon cabin. Despite John's pleading and explanation, he was forcefully separated from his bride and was never allowed to retain her as his wife.

Sam Hargrove would have his hands full with his new acquisition. When Jasper took up his duties in Hargrove's tobacco factory, he was described as "a wild sinner, full of dangerous energies, utterly without fear of God. He moved at a perilous pace, making evil things fearfully fascinating, rushing headlong into perdition."

Jasper ran in rebellion for five years before the Hound of Heaven and Tina Jasper's prayers caught up with him. Tina was joined by a small band of saints who lined the tobacco-laden tables in the factory where John worked. While hands were occupied with the limp brown leaves, minds soared aloft, petitioning Heaven for John's salvation.

Sam Hargrove, too, who contradicts our caricature of slaveholders as insufferable tyrants, was among those who prayed for Jasper.

By his own account, he was brought to bay beneath the old clock tower in Richmond's Capitol Square. It was the Fourth of July in 1839. Jasper was celebrating his birthday by mingling with slaves and citizens who were enjoying the commemorative festivities.

"I was sittin' there on a bench under the cool shade. Folks was swarmin' around and laughin' and hurrahin' when, quick as lightnin', God's arrow of conviction went into my proud heart and brought me low."

The wounded rebel staggered along for six weeks before the divine shaft brought him down. "Just because," he lamented, "I was such a fool I couldn't see the way."

John was standing at a table in the factory, stemming tobacco on a sultry summer morning. "The darkness of death," he would remember, "was in my soul. My sins were piled on me like a mountain; my feet were sinkin' down in the regions of despair. I thought I would die right then, and with what I supposed was my last breath, I flung up a cry to Heaven for mercy.

"Before I knew it the light broke; I was light as a feather; my feet were on the mountain; salvation rolled like a flood through my soul."

John attempted to muzzle his joy, fearing trouble from the overseer. Looking up the long rows of tables, he saw an elderly believer "who loved me," he explained, "and had tried hard to lead me out of the darkness." The infant Christian "slipped 'round to where he was," and said in his ear, as low as he could, "Hallelujah! My soul is redeemed!"

That was enough. Praiseful pandemonium broke out among the slave laborers as the dusty air reverberated with the exclamation, "Jasper's got religion!"

Jasper had more that "religion." What the uproar got him was a quick summons to Master Sam's office.

He entered with some trepidation—it was no light thing to distract people from their work. When John had finished his explanation, Hargrove spoke "with a pretty little quiver in his voice," Jasper recalled.

"John, I believe that way myself. I love the Savior you have just found," and Hargrove extended a hand. "I wish you well. Your Savior is mine, and we are now brothers in the Lord."

Master Sam then asked, "John did you tell many of them out there about your conversion?" He had told only two face-to-face. "Go tell 'em, John," Hargrove said. "Go back in there and go up and down the tables, and tell all of them. Tell everybody what the Lord has done for you."

So Sam Hargrove's chattel became the bond servant of Jesus Christ, and over the next 62 years he would be faithful to the charge to "go tell 'em."

Jasper wanted to learn all he could about Christ and the Bible, but he was unable to read. The Lord's answer to his problem came in the person of William Jackson. Jackson not only knew how to read, he also possessed a ragged *New York Speller*. The two men became roommates and began their labor in learning. Seven months later, John could read his Bible.

His eagerness to learn the Word and share the truth was not lost on Hargrove. When John began to demonstrate a gift for preaching, Hargrove granted him time away from his duties to pursue his opportunities to minister.

Like his father, John did his early preaching at funerals for slaves. Blacks were permitted to select one of their own to bring a short message after the white clergyman had finished his address.

Jasper exhibited God-given flashes of sanctified eloquence while filling one of his first engagements. He visualized the deceased, who had been a sincere believer, "with eyes uplifted and a smile that would cover an acre of ugliness."

Jasper pointed to the skies. "Look at him, brethren! Look at him enterin' Glory, just like a conquerin' Roman! See those white horses drawin' his chariot! See that palm of victory! See his white garment!" Before many months had passed, Jasper was the premier funeral preacher in the Old Dominion.

By the time the long night of slavery faded and blacks blinked their way into the brilliance of freedom's morning, John Jasper had been preaching for 25 years. A free man at last, he was ready, at 53 years of age, to begin living out his long-cherished dream of becoming a pastor.

His first problem as a free man was providing food for the table. The initial opportunity for employment came with an offer to clean bricks from buildings that had been destroyed by the Union forces. The job paid 50 cents per thousand.

He began to gather a congregation in a converted stable on Brown's Island in the James River. Nine people attended. Before long, however, they were forced to vacate in favor of a larger building, one once used as a carpenter's shop. Two years after the church was founded, they purchased the brick building on Duval Street that was to permanently house the Sixth Mount Zion Baptist Church—John Jasper, pastor.

Richmond soon took notice of what was happening in the Jackson Ward section of "little Africa." Week after week, Pastor Jasper led processions of believers to the James for baptismal services. On one Sunday afternoon, he immersed more than three hundred converts.

The former slave was an unlikely candidate to become one of the most respected and revered men on either side of the color line in Richmond. At a time in life when some men are beginning to forget what they have learned, Jasper was, in many respects, starting his education. "I crept along mighty tedious, gettin' a crumb here and there," he said.

In the initial phases of his ministry, he knew little about doctrine, theology, and pastoring. The man who was barely literate himself was forced into educating his desperately needy people.

Jasper wrestled with the temptation from old vices that attempted to bring him down. "I been havin' my temptations all my life," he confessed, "and I have them yet, a heap of them, and some of them are very bad."

Still another struggle emanated from the personal insecurity that often taunts men who feel inadequately prepared. He often became defensive and militant when challenged by critics.

John needed help. His eloquence and rudimentary grasp of the Scriptures drew hungry-hearted people to Christ by the score, but he needed to learn more. God sent him Dr. William Eldridge Hatcher, pastor of the Grace Baptist Church, Richmond's largest white congregation.

When Hatcher began to attend Jasper's Sunday afternoon services, a practice he would continue for 20 years, people at Grace Baptist criticized their pastor. "Jasper's English is horrible," they complained.

"So it is," Hatcher responded, "but I do not go to listen to Jasper's English. I go to hear him talk about his Jesus."

Hatcher went to Jasper to get his heart warmed; Jasper came to Hatcher's study to get his head filled with doctrine. The result was apparent.

John had his own method of sermon preparation. "First, I read my Bible until a text gets a hold on me. Then I go down to the James River and walk it in. Then I go into my pulpit and preach it out."

He did not hesitate to repeat sermons he had *walked in.* "There are some sermons," he explained, "I like to hear myself preach again, and what blesses me blesses others." His members, eventually numbering more than two thousand, knew some of his messages almost as well as he did. But their familiarity only seemed to heighten anticipation.

The fundamental strength of Jasper's preaching, however, was not in fervor, phrases, or repetition. Said the editor of the *Richmond Planet*, "He believed in putting the truth where it could be easily reached and plainly understood."

When he preached, Jasper had a way of robing the truth in descriptive eloquence. He wove before his hearers multihued verbal tapestries bearing intricate patterns of the heavenly landscape. To hear him expound God's Word was to see what he was saying.

During a funeral address, Jasper bent over, cupped his hands to his mouth, and called down to the monarch of the lower regions: "Grave! Grave! Oh Grave! Where is your victory? I hear you got a mighty banner down there, and you terrorize everybody who comes along that way. Bring out your armies and furl forth your banners of victory. Show your hand and let 'em see what you can do."

Then he made the grave reply: "Ain't got no victory down here now; had victory, but King Jesus passed through this country an' tore my banners down. He says His people won't be troubled no more, an' He told me to open the gates an' let 'em pass on their way to Glory."

"Oh my brethren," Jasper exclaimed, "did you hear that? My Jesus jerked the sting from death, broke the scepter of the king of terrors, and He went into the grave and robbed it of its victorious banners. He fixed a way nice and smooth for His people to pass through. More than that, He has written a song, a shoutin' anthem for us to sing when we go out there, passin' suns and stars, and singin' that song. 'Thanks be unto God, who gives us victory through the Lord Jesus Christ.' "

White people came in large numbers to hear him preach. Many were prominent figures of the era, including Douglas Southall Freeman, historian and biographer of Robert E. Lee, and Edward W. Hudgins, chief justice of the Supreme Court of Appeals. On one occasion, the entire Virginia Legislature attended.

As custom was, black parishioners gave up their seats to the guests. Many Sixth Mount Zion members stood in the overflow to hear snatches of the sermon.

Jasper could be dull—sermons often ran well over an hour—but that was the exception. More often, world-weary saints were cheered by the challenge.

"Nothin' short of the pearly gates can satisfy me," he exhorted. "And I charge you, my people, fix your feet on the Solid Rock, your hearts on Calvary, your eyes on the throne of the Lamb. These strifes will soon be over; we shall see the King in His glory and be at ease in Zion. Go on! Go on! Ye ransomed of the Lord."

Sinners were always warned, and Jasper didn't spare the living or the dead in getting the message across. At one funeral service he said, "Let me say a word about this William Ellyson. I say it first to get it off my mind. He was no good man. He didn't say he was. He didn't try to be good. It's a bad tale to tell on him, but he fixed the story himself. He died as he lived—without God an' without hope in this world. If you want folks preached an' sung into Glory, don't bring them to Jasper. My task is to comfort the mourner an' warn the unruly."

Jasper's greatest controversy came over his most famous sermon, "The Sun Do Move." He believed that Scripture proved that the sun moved around the earth. He came to the pulpit armed with verses he felt would settle the issue. The sermon received undue attention and brought a volatile rebuke from some of the black clergy in Richmond.

Three of their number were grieved to the point of publishing a response to the message in the local newspapers. "We enter," they wrote, "a solemn protest against all such base fabrications."

Jasper, never one to yield to fear of the opposition, took up the gauntlet. "What saucy tongues these educated, kid-gloved preachers have," he observed. The comment was perhaps the mildest word he had for his critics.

In the end, his besieged adversaries ran up the white flag. "We desire," they acknowledged publicly, "to change the phrase 'base fabrications.' We do not hold Jasper's views, but we extend him and his church a fraternal hand."

The argument never diminished his parishioners' respect and admiration for their pastor. To the best of his ability, they were certain, he would always tell them the truth as he saw it in the Word of God.

On a Sunday in May 1901, the frail patriarch ascended his cherished pulpit for the last time. "My words are for my brethren, my church," he said. "They are the people for whose souls I watch. For them I got to stand an' report at the last day. They are my sheep, an' I am their shepherd, an' my soul is knit with them forever."

Knowing that death was imminent, he explained his situation in true Jasperian fashion: "I am now at the river's bank an' waitin' for further orders."

Death Meets The Master

This poem is based on a passage from one of John Jasper's sermons on the resurrection.

Father Time met Pale King Death
    Sittin' by a tomb.
"Hello, old friend. I guess you're here
    To seal somebody's doom."

"You might say that," sly Death replied—
    A smile slid up his face.
"Inside repose that Jesus man
    Who said He'd save the race.

"And you, Time, why you stoppin' here?
    Don't you have things to do?"
"I come each day to draw the veil
    And let the mornin' through.

"Say, why you watchin' jus' one grave
    With all your vast domain?
Looks like you'd be out ramblin' 'round
    An' smitin' folks with pain."

"Oh, this one's somethin' special,
    He challenged me they say.
Said He'd rest here just three days
    Then stir and walk away.

"Now I'm the Conqueror you know,
    They don't talk up to me.
When I step in to cut 'em down
    It's for eternity."

"I sure can testify to that,"
    Responded Father Time,
"I ain't seen one shake off the dust
    Since you been in your prime.

"Well, I've got other things to do,
　　I must be on my way.
I'll see you when I come back by
　　To make another day."

So whiskered Time went up the hill
　　To bid the sun to rise,
And left Death standin' by the tomb
　　Lookin' strong and wise.

Next day, Time ambled by again,
　　"An' how are things?" he queried.
"Kinda quiet," Death replied,
　　"I'm startin' to be wearied.

"Won't be here when you come by
　　About this time tomorrow.
I'm anxious to be on my way
　　To spread some grief an' sorrow."

Now Father Time was quite surprised
　　When he came back to see
Death a-quiverin' on the ground
　　In frightful agony!

His eyes were set; his throat was marked;
　　His clothes in disarray.
It wasn't difficult to see:
　　Old Death had had his day.

"What happened Death?" asked Father Time,
　　"What makes you look so bad?
I've never seen you shake this way
　　Or seem so scared and sad."

Death pulled himself up on a rock
　　Lookin' sick and humble.
Hung his head an' wrung his hands,
　　Then Time could hear him mumble.

"Was sittin' here before the dawn,
  About to take my stroll,
When all at once this whole wide world
  Began to reel and roll.

"That rollin' stone jumped off the door
  An' skipped on down the hill.
Then everything grew dark and quiet,
  Seemed like the world stood still.

"I saw Him standin' in the door—
  He didn't move or speak,
Just looked at me an' all at once
  I felt so tired and weak.

"He came and got a hold on me
  An' threw me to the ground.
Put His foot here on my neck,
  Then took my keys and crown.

"Two angels came to talk with Him,
  They glistened like the sun.
He said, 'The plan's all finished now,
  Redemption's work is done.'

"An' as they passed the garden gate
  I heard Him say, just then,
He's setting free my captives,
  And givin' gifts to men."

Time and Death met once again
  Off yonder by the gate.
"It's good to see you," said old Time,
  "I've wondered 'bout your fate."

"Oh, I'm a lowly servant now,
  There's little time to roam.
I just push open this old gate,
  And help the saints go home!"

Stonewall Jackson's Bible

"The fame of Stonewall Jackson is no longer the exclusive property of Virginia and the South, it has become the birthright of every person privileged to call himself an American."

This sweeping tribute by Field Marshall Viscount Garnet Wolseley of the British Army in memory of a man raised in near obscurity is a testimonial to the impact of the renowned general's life. When we realize how few men have dominated the minds of their contemporaries as did Thomas Jonathan Jackson, it is well that we take some time to find out why this was true.

Stonewall Jackson was an enigma to most of his peers, and the passing of more than a century has not diminished the perplexity encountered while reading accounts of his life. Indeed, some of the men who have written biographies of the great Civil War general seem to have missed the true substance of his life entirely. He is often portrayed as a strange, brooding eccentric, a mystical sort who, while he commanded the gods of war as few men have, was driven by a religious fanaticism bordering dementia. These men may stand in awe of the military genius of Jackson, but they have never really come to know the man—a failing which can be attributed to the fact that there is such a vast area of his life which is hidden from the view of an unspiritual observer. In fact, General Jackson was so totally dominated by God and a sense of divine purpose that only those people of like mind can rightly interpret his life.

Born in Clarksville, Virginia (now West Virginia), Jackson was orphaned at the age of three. The first years of his life were spent in privation and hardship. His spiritual situation was even more barren. At 18 he received the appointment to West Point which proved to be the first great turning point in his life. It was while at the academy that another young cadet decided to share his faith in Jesus Christ with young Jackson. He told him of the love of God in Christ and how God had transformed his own life. The young man's witness became a seed in good ground. From that point the future general began a long period of inquiry about religions and Christianity that culminated in his public profession of faith in the Presbyterian Church in Lexington, Virginia. From the moment he trusted Christ, Jackson became a thoroughly transformed individual.

He immediately became a man of the Bible. God's Word became the *Bread of Heaven* to him. Consequently, he came to believe one could find every need of life met within the confines of its pages. One day, he informed a young staff officer, a man named Smith, that he could find an answer to virtually everything in the Bible. "Do you know where you find campaign strategy in the Bible?" queried Jackson. "Why, no," was the rather embarrassed reply. Jackson smiled. "Study Joshua!" Stonewall had studied Joshua with a determination to apply what he learned from the illustrious Old Testament commander.

It is a tribute to Stonewall's mastery of tactical maneuvers that the greatest soldiers of modern times have traveled to America to study his campaigns. They trekked the valleys of Virginia in the wake of Jackson and his flying gray legions. He, before them, had followed in the train of Joshua and, in so doing, became the wonder of the military world.

Often, when his wife Anna would read to him, he would say, "Mark that." She dutifully underlined the prescribed passages in their family Bibles, and Jackson carefully referred to them in future encounters with the Book.

Some years ago, a pastor friend told me that these Bibles were kept in the Jackson home, which now serves as a museum, in Lexington, Virginia. On a visit to the home I requested and received permission from the curator to examine them and record some of the verses marked for posterity.

The Bibles were indeed penciled and display an amazing degree of consistency with the life Stonewall Jackson lived during his appointed time on earth. They leave an eloquent, silent memorial to the power of the Word when it is translated in a submissive heart.

We will note some of these marked verses and harmonize them with events in the General's life.

And we know that all things work together for good to them that love God, to them who are the called according to his purpose (Rom. 8:28).

This verse was shared with Chaplain Lacy at Guinea Station just before his death. Jackson had been accidentally wounded by one of his own troops at Chancellorsville. The verse clearly reveals the life-view of the soldier-saint. He believed that God had a distinct program for his life. In the will of God, he was immortal while there was still work to be done. He explained: "My religious beliefs teach me to feel as safe in battle as in bed!"

"Not my will, but thine be done," was another quotation often used by Jackson. The phrase "thine be done" reflected accurately his commitment to the Lordship of Jesus Christ.

In victory he was always quick to give credit to the Lord. His journals are filled with sayings such as, "God has given a great victory today" and "Our Heavenly Father blesses us exceedingly."

When General Robert E. Lee wrote a note of congratulation on his great victory at Chancellorsville, Jackson replied, "General Lee is very kind to me, but he should give the glory to God."

One of his most quoted sayings, "Never take counsel with your fears," is a prime example of the aggressiveness of his faith. In fact, he never did take counsel with his fears, nor should we, if His will is ours.

Render to Caesar the things that are Caesar's . . . (Mk. 12:17a).

There are those who cannot reconcile the fierceness of the warrior with the meekness of the Christ-life. Jackson did not see any incompatibility between the two. He viewed life as a unity which was not compartmentalized into areas drawn along secular and sacred lines. Duty to country became a responsibility to God. Patriotism and loyalty to the cause in which he believed were to be pursued with the same vigor as was his worship. As a soldier he could say, "War means fighting and the business of a soldier is to fight." Because of this singular devotion to the demands of his profession, some have pictured him as a frenzied ogre who fed on war, battles, and death. Nothing could be more inaccurate. "It is painful to me," he lamented, "to discover with what unconcern they talk of war and threaten it. I have seen enough of it to make me look upon it as the sum of all evils." But obedience to God involved obedience to his country. Loyalty to Christ, in Jackson's mind, had to be equated to the cause he served.

. . . and to God the things that are God's (Mk. 12:17b).

Few people realize the seriousness with which the general viewed Christian work. A friend in Lexington once asked if he had ever considered missionary service in Africa. "If God called me to go to Africa, I'd go without my hat." He commented further, "I should not be surprised were I to die upon a foreign field clad in ministerial armour fighting under the banner of Jesus." So here we see a man with unsurpassed loyalty to his cause, yet one who was marching to the drum of his supreme Commander, Jesus Christ.

Jackson was a meticulous tither. He cautioned his wife to give a tenth, or more, to Christian work. He kept an account of his giving. Some listed items include: "Ladies Missionary Society, $2.00; Davidson College $1.00; the poor, $1.10; Bible Society, $2.00; Foreign Missions, $5.00; Parsonage Fund, $25.00."

The seemingly disproportionate amount for the building of a parsonage may have been a form of penance in partial payment for his inescapable malady of falling asleep while his pastor was preaching. He had a habit of sitting bolt upright in full view of other worshipers. When overtaken by his infirmity during chapel services at Virginia Military Institute, he became the object of some uncomplimentary remarks and no small amount of snickering ridicule from the cadets. When encouraged by a fellow professor to assume a less conspicuous posture during these encounters with Morpheus, Jackson replied that he must bear the indignity of his transgression, and, if students saw him asleep in chapel, he would be obliged to suffer his shame publicly.

And, as Moses lifted up the serpent in the wilderness, even so must the Son of man be lifted up, That whosoever believeth in him should not perish, but have eternal life. For God so loved the world, that he gave his only begotten Son, that whosoever believeth in him should not perish, but have everlasting life (Jn. 3:14-16).

That at the name of Jesus every knee should bow . . . And that every tongue should confess that Jesus Christ is Lord, to the glory of God, the Father (Phil. 2:10-11).

Paul's familiar words embody the irrepressible evangelistic fervor which so dominated Stonewall Jackson's life. The message of the gospel was the heartbeat of his soul. "It is a glorious thing to be a minister of the Gospel of the Prince of Peace: there is no equal position in all the world." Not only did he believe this to be true, he participated in the proclamation of the gospel message at every opportunity. Evangelistic meetings were a regular occurrence in his camp. He recruited chaplains for his men who evidenced the power of God on their ministries. In evaluating qualifications for chaplains, it was Jackson's contention that "In the Army no question should be asked as to the denomination a chaplain belongs. Let the question be: 'Does he preach the Gospel?' "

One day the revered commander ambled into an artillery encampment in search of a certain corporal. Stonewall carried a brown package he wished to deliver. The corporal was not to be found so the parcel was left in his tent. Speculation swept the camp. Why would Stonewall Jackson seek out a lowly corporal with a gift? Perhaps this was an unexpected promotion or an expensive reward for some act of valor. When the young celebrity returned, his eager companions gathered to view the opening of the mysterious package. It contained gospel tracts to be distributed among the artillerymen.

His love for personal witness is reflected in his relationship with General Richard S. Ewell, who joined Jackson's command as a notoriously profane man. Ewell initially viewed his superior officer as quite insane and did not hesitate to air his views before his intimates. His attitude soon changed, and Jackson seemed to take special pains to bear witness to his fellow soldier. Once, after a battle, he took Ewell aside for some time and pointed out what he interpreted as evidences of God's intervention on their behalf. The conversation ended with Jackson's exclamation to Ewell, "If a man can't see the hand of God in this, he is blind!"

The warrior of infamous reputation for his volatile vocabulary left the service at the close of the war as a humble Christian. Stonewall Jackson's testimony for Christ played a major role in Ewell's conversion.

While in Lexington, the general founded and taught a large Sunday School for blacks. He wrote his sister, "I do rejoice to walk in the love of God my heavenly Father. I'm rejoiced that He has condescended to use me as an instrument for setting up a large Sabbath School for negroes here." The joy of his heart was to minister the Word of God to his class. It was ever in his mind. During the battle of First Manassas (Bull Run), Jackson wrote a hurried letter to his pastor, Dr. William S. White. "Dear Pastor: I remember that I failed to send my contribution for our colored Sunday School. Enclosed you will find my check." While the thunder of war rattled about him, and the history of the nation was in traumatic evolution, the heart of this man turned toward those who were loved in the Lord.

Therefore, I say unto you, Whatever things ye desire, when ye pray, believe that ye receive them, and ye shall have them (Mk. 11:24).

Thomas Jackson had a simple, childlike quality when he petitioned his Lord in prayer. Dr. Stiles, an eminent minister of the day, said of him: "He came nearer putting God in God's place than any man we have ever known."

Jackson's prayer life manifested refreshing dimensions. Early in his Christian experience he dedicated himself to the practice of prayer. Public prayer, however, was a special trial for the reticent professor. He was once called on to pray in a public meeting at his church. He rose to his feet, stammered, then expelled short utterances punctuated by long, silent intervals. The pastor became embarrassed for the struggling brother. Members of the congregation shifted uneasily, waiting for the ordeal to conclude. At the close of the service the pastor offered his apologies and promised not to call on him again. Jackson protested strenuously. "No, no. I must learn to address my God in public." And keep at it he did until later in his life a preacher named Ewing crowned him with the supreme compliment. "He did not pray to men," Ewing observed, "but to God."

Prayer was as regular as sunrise in his camp—so much so that the famed artist Vizetelly made a prayer meeting with the general and his men the subject of a now-famous engraving.

Of personal prayer, he said, "I have so fixed the habit in my mind that I never raise a glass of water to my lips without a moment's asking of God's blessing. I never seal a letter without pasting a word of prayer under the seal. The habit is as fixed in me as breathing."

He explained how he observed the scriptural admonition to "pray without ceasing." Jackson prayed when he rose from his bed, and while he walked to the classroom. As the cadets were taking their seats, he would ask God's blessing upon them and His guidance in the activities of the day. When classes were over he prayed his way home. Later, he sealed the night watch with a time of intimate communion with his Lord.

Perhaps the most penetrating comment on the power of the general's prayer was made by Henry Kyd Douglas, the youngest member of Jackson's staff. "It is a singular thing that General Jackson, while living, never had a staff member killed or wounded until Chancellorsville, where he fell, and as he never spared them or himself, it was often remarked upon. After the protection of his presence and prayers had been withdrawn, death played havoc with them."

And he said to them all, If any man will come after me, let him deny himself, and take up his cross daily, and follow me (Lk. 9:23).

Stonewall Jackson practiced self-discipline as few men have. He believed it a part of his duty to set a proper example for his men. Because of this belief, he never took a leave after he entered active service. He returned to his home in Lexington only in death. A Colonel Henderson, writing about Jackson years later, stated, "Ten thousand soldiers learned self-denial which is the root of all manliness. Strength and simplicity of childlike faith and most fiery energy [were learned from him]."

His unfailing example gave birth to a deep love and boundless loyalty among the men in gray who followed him. To be a member of the famed Stonewall Brigade was something akin to coronation. So compelling was his influence that a federal officer was moved to write:

> And men will tell their children
>   When all other memories fade
> How they fought with Stonewall Jackson
>   In the old Stonewall Brigade.
> And oft in dreams his fierce brigade
>   Shall see the form they followed far—
> Still leading in the farthest van—
>   A landmark in the cloud of war.
> And oft when white-haired grandsires tell
>   Of bloody struggles past and gone,
> The children at their knees will hear
>   How Jackson led his columns on!

Years after the war ended in 1865, confederate veterans converged on Richmond for the unveiling and dedication of the statue of General Robert E. Lee. Next morning, a row of men wrapped in gray blankets were seen sleeping around the statue of General Jackson in Capitol Square. As the gray-haired sleepers rose, a passing citizen called out to them, "Were there no beds in Richmond last night?" One of the elderly veterans replied, "Oh, yes, there were plenty of places, but we were his boys and we wanted to sleep with the old man just once more."

Behold, I show you a mystery: We shall not all sleep, but we shall all be changed, In a moment, in the twinkling of an eye, at the last trump ... O death, where is thy sting? O grave, where is thy victory? (1 Cor. 15:51–52, 55).

For we know that if our earthly house of this tabernacle were dissolved, we have a building of God, an house not made with hands, eternal in the heavens (2 Cor. 5:1).

Thomas Jonathan Jackson possessed a bold assurance of our sure hope. As he rode his little steed across the battlefields of this world, he looked with eagerness toward the day when he would serve under the visible banner of the King of his life, Jesus Christ. He met the great archadversary of humanity with sublime confidence. His parting words were, "Let us cross over the river and rest under the shade of the trees." Jackson was as victorious in death as he had been in life. He could proclaim with another sainted warrior, "I have finished my course, I have kept the faith" (2 Tim. 4:7).

Another of the marked verses will provide an appropriate closing word.

And the peace of God, which passeth all understanding, shall keep your hearts and minds through Christ Jesus (Phil. 4:7).

Going Home

Frequent separation from the family is the downside of itinerant work. I often think how difficult it must be for missionaries who, in the will of God, must bear the trial of being distanced from relatives and children for long periods of time. Holidays, especially, activate my homing mechanism and bring about acute spasms of homesickness.

I was coming home a few years ago following fall meetings. It had been a long season, and I was feeling the effects of travel and extended separation from the family. Christmas was almost upon us, and the inner pressure to get home was increasingly intense. As I drove through a depressed section of West Virginia, I suddenly felt as though I were on a concrete treadmill that was taking me nowhere—a sensation not unknown to frequent travelers. But as my mind settled down, I was refreshed to realize that this road was not fashioned for a perpetual experience. It had been laid to take people like me home.

All roads are made to end at a desired destination. That's true in this life. But the great comfort is to be found in the fact that, for the believer, all earthly roads merge with the one that ends before our permanent residence in Heaven.

Roads Are Made To End

Every road is made to end,
I'm glad for that today.
I couldn't bear another mile,
If it were not that way.
December's throwing sloppy snow,
And gray haze shrouds each hill.
The trees stand nude and frozen,
Erect but deathly still.
Smoke curls from a cabin flue,
Forlorn as those inside.
Dirt and cold and poverty
Have come there to abide.
Dancing Christmas lights I see
In distant windows clear.
"Get on Home," they call to me,
"You've got no business here."
This road will end where warmth and love
And song have settled down,
Atop a quiet little rise
On the outskirts of our town.
I won't budge till calendars turn
On a year called "New";
Then back out on the empty road.
Does that seem sad to you?
No.
Every one of them will end
Where folk need what I bring—
A road, however long or dark,
Becomes a welcome thing.

Thanksgiving 1984

It's Thanksgiving,
   And I'm going home.
That's the best thing
   In my world today.

I've been gone too long;
   I'm tired inside.
But that will end
   When we turn up our drive.

They'll all be there,
   So for a little while
Things will seem just
   Like they used to be.

Better, really, for those
   Grandson scamps
Will be around to wrestle,
   Pick and tease.

Mom will show her genius
   In the pies,
And stuffing mortal
   Tongue cannot describe.

We'll laugh ourselves tired
   Before we're through;
But this is tired
   Of another kind.

Weariness with quiet
   In the soul.
It's Thanksgiving,
   And I'm home again!

Stages of Life

The way seemed long at morning's light
   With many a mile to go;
But He was there to walk with me
   Through darkest vales below.

High noon found the sun white-hot
   And twisting heights to scale;
But He was there with quiet word:
   "With Me you cannot fail."

At evening I felt tired and old
   So wearied with the way;
But He was there with steadying hand—
   His strength became my stay.

Night came with a numbing chill
   And I fell pale and cold;
Then with His arms He lifted me
   And took me to His fold.

Here Alone

To every thing there is a season, and a time to every purpose under the heaven: A time to be born, and a time to die . . . A time to weep, and a time to laugh . . . a time to keep silence, and a time to speak (Eccl. 3:1b, 2, 4, 7b).

Most of us find it difficult to express ourselves to friends who have lost a loved one in death. I remember vividly my feelings, as a young minister, after what I felt was a failed attempt to comfort a family who had lost a child through tragic circumstances. I stood outside the funeral home in the darkness wondering why I didn't have the right words to say. Oh, I had words and Bible verses, but it seemed to me they didn't break through to their need at all. I came to understand over the years, however, that there are times when no one can say anything that will ease the pain and anguish felt in such circumstances. Just being there seems to say with some eloquence what tongues cannot adequately convey: "I'm here, and I care, and I'll share your time for weeping."

A pastor friend of mine had experienced the sudden home-going of his wife. When the church secretary called to ask about motel arrangements for a conference I was to conduct at his church, I told her I would like to stay at the parsonage. "Well," she said, "you know he's there alone. You two will have to batch it." "I know," I replied, "that's the reason I prefer this arrangement."

For several days my friend and I rattled around a large house that now seemed frightfully empty. It was then I came face-to-face with the full realization that only the Lord Himself can minister effectively to our deepest needs in what must be life's most difficult time of transition.

She's gone from me, and I am here alone.
　　Her life is past, but I must stay awhile.
Going home is hardest, I suppose,
　　Of all the empty tasks that I now face.
It's dark there and frost is on the panes;
　　Echoes sound where cozy snugness reigned.
I sit before a table sparsely set,
　　And stir up ripples in my coffee cup.
I listen, but silence owns this day.
　　I think I'll go away to find some place
Where no one knows or cares what we once had.
　　Maybe then it won't hurt quite so much.
Perhaps in time the light will come again.
　　No, I can't leave—it wouldn't help.
I'd be no nearer to her far away.
　　I'll look for solace where I found it first,
When He came in to fill my empty world.
　　I'll just contemplate His word to me:
"You're not alone, I'll fill her place," He says.
　　So over lonely hours that lie ahead,
I'll turn to Him for what I need just then.
　　And whether someone comes to grace my days
Or I stay here to walk these halls alone,
　　My rest will be in His behest to me
To daily dispel all my loneliness.

Words from An Old Graveyard

Our son, Andy, is a fine amateur photographer. His admiration for the work of the late Ansel Adams has brought numerous books and calendars of the master photographer's labor into my possession. A treasured picture is a moonrise over an old graveyard in Hernandez, New Mexico.

Graveyards in the old west, unlike dignified cemeteries or modern memorial parks, are places where people went to great lengths to say sad things in humorous ways. Boot Hill in Tombstone, Arizona, provides a classic example.

> Here lies
> Lester Moore
> four slugs
> from a forty-four
> no Les
> no more

Often, too, they tell tragic tales which spring from deprivation and disease-riddled circumstances with terse pathos, as in the case of several infant graves filled from a single family marked simply, "Too soon gone."

In the New Mexico graveyard, however, Adams captured an almost singular expression. A pale moon hangs above craggy mountains hauntingly streaked by deftly layered cloud formations. Sparse vegetation breaks the desert around an adobe church and a few simple buildings. The graveyard is surrounded by a rickety fence which appears quite indifferent to its assigned duty. Cement headstones and crude wooden crosses, some tilted at precarious angles, stand the watch over small squares where other people from other times placed the bodies of their dead. The entire scene has a beckoning quality—as if it has something to say to those of us who linger here.

What does this silent graveyard
    wish to say to me?
"You're mortal! Moving, ever moving,
    toward the dust.
Your feet are in it already, and soon your
    fragile body will be too.
Time and dust will prevail."

But that's only half the story,
Because I'm more than feet in
    dust and mud.
I'm head, and heart, and hands—
    soul and spirit—
Made for realms flung high above this earth.
My heart and head are there already.
And after I've lingered here to do His bidding
    for a time,
I'll move through this old graveyard
    on the journey to my homeland
        ever so far beyond the stars.

Cemeteries

Mother and I walked through the town cemetery I had so soundly feared as a child growing up in Michigan. I had heard all of the stories that strike fear into boys with small misdeeds on their consciences. "If you whistle when you go by," I had been solemnly advised, "nothin's apt to get you." I tried it a few times, but I soon decided that a hard run outdid a good whistle any day of the week. But on this day, years removed from those fearsome apparitions, things seemed very different. As a child this had been foreign territory—names faintly known but never attached to real persons. People were now connected to those names. Relatives, schoolmates, and friends, many of whom were much younger than I when they died, were among the names on the silent monuments. I thought about how much smaller my earthly circle was growing while the heavenly "cloud of witnesses" was getting larger. Cemeteries aren't such bad places after all.

Cemeteries used to bother me.
　　They seemed so foreign to my life and times.
Their occupants came from another world—
　　Old dates on mossy granite with verses hard to read.

But they look very different to me now.
　　I walk among some friends who've left this place.
Their tents are folded, neatly laid aside
　　In silent rows beneath bronze epitaphs.

One day—soon I think—these tabernacles will arise
　　As habitations for another sphere.
Temples this time, like His very own,
　　To house a people resting with Him now.

So thoughts of liberation come to me,
　　For when I lay my tattered shelter down,
You all will come to place it with the rest,
　　While raised on wings of peace I'll fly to God.

Who Needs Heaven

We don't hear much about Heaven these days.

Perhaps it's because most of us don't really feel we need Heaven. Much of our energy seems to be spent in instructing or learning to be well-adjusted in this world.

We smile at quaint spirituals about golden slippers, swooping chariots, and cabins to be exchanged for mansions in glory.

Maybe we need to give some thought to the people who sang those songs. They were ill-clad, dusky captives in a strange land, people who walked frost-covered paths, seeking wood for fires to beat back winter's numbing cold from crack-laced cabin doors. Their lives were blighted by enforced servitude, separations, "trials and tribulations."

They sang about the time when morning would come and a heavenly chariot would swing low, snatching their fleeing spirits away to that land of eternal day. There they would walk, God-shod, resplendent in heavenly vestments, stepping down golden avenues toward mansions warmed by the radiance of the Lamb.

They longed for home.

And they admitted that they were aliens and strangers on earth. People who say such things show that they are looking for a country of their own. If they had been thinking of the country they had left, they would have had the opportunity to return. Instead, they were longing for a better country—a heavenly one.

Therefore God is not ashamed to be called their God, for he has prepared a city for them.

The world was not worthy of them (Heb. 11:13–16, 38 NIV).

They needed Heaven.

If

If all our dreams and hopes
    were bound by earth and time,
If all our lives were fading,
    frail todays,
Then even crowned with robust
    length of years,
Our lives would prove a pilgrimage
    of tears.
All the good, the best that this
    world gave,
Would end in muted dirges at
    the grave.

If all our dreams and hopes
    are fixed on Jesus Christ,
If all our lives are rooted
    in His Word,
Then all that's bright in life
    looms fairer still
As we become the subjects
    of His will.

And when my bark shall quit life's
    stream where once it meets the sea,
There Savior, loved ones, sainted friends
    will wait to welcome me.

Pillars
Revelation 3:12

People pass by pillars standing
    Silent, straight, and tall.
Some will pause to notice them;
    Most never look at all.

Truth is, pillars don't call out
    And tell how grand they are,
But standing speak of strength so true
    It passes words by far.

Pillars just keep standing fast,
    While folk dash to and fro.
Unaffected by the din—
    They do more than we know.

Pillars keep our structures
    From falling on our heads.
Watch to give us safety
    While we rest on our beds.

God loves pillars—
    Chooses them to teach us what is true.
Then lets us stand beside them
    To learn what we should do.

He used a fiery pillar
    To lead His children home.
Without it only wilderness
    So aimlessly to roam.

Pillars of stone directed
    Simple worship toward the skies
To rise before their Sovereign
    In the place where no one dies.

Great pillars stood as sentinels
    At Tabernacle door
To open paths to peace with God—
    Could any ask for more?

Frank was a pillar tall and true,
    Who stood to help us on,
But like most pillars, we'll take note
    The more because he's gone.

For Gordon
1 Corinthians 15:10

He was our friend,
    But so much more than that,
This Gordon we have just
    Watched go away.
He grew old;
    But he never was old.
It does sound strange
    A thing like this to say.

His life was in the Book,
    That kept him young.
And he had things to do
    For you and me.
He urged us: "Help me get
    These Bibles out.
The Book's man's only source
    Of light, you see."

The people of that Book,
    They held his heart
With grip so strong
    They would not let him go.
And every day he told us,
    Once again,
About the Jews,
    And how God loves them so.

Yes, there's another soldier
    For the line
To step into his place
    And help us through.
But I guess He really
    Won't be quite the same.
For there was just one Gordon
    Prepared for me and you.

Old Men and Young Men

Fred and Leslie were old men in a place frequented by young marrieds and their children. I watched them one day as they sat on a bench beside a pond in rural New Hampshire. Like ancient Athenian philosophers, they squinted against the sun, gestured, and nodded as their conversation brushed this issue or that. These men, I thought, come from a different world than the one known to the young men playing around them or walking past. But, I concluded, when it comes to the things that really matter, their worlds aren't so different after all.

Old men talk
Of yesterday;
The young reach
For tomorrow.
One thing sure
For young and old:
They'll know their
Share of sorrow.

Life has a way
Of beating men,
And leaving them
To wonder
About the reason
For it all,
The quiet and
The thunder.

For there are
Few among the old
Who've done more
Than survive,
Who just keep
Getting up again—
Bloodied, but alive.

Some live in desperate
Solitude,
Some bitter,
Insecure.
Some look for love
They cannot find,
And some are just
Not sure.

The young think
They can change it all.
"Life won't beat us,"
They cry.
But watch their faces
Through the years
And see their bright
Hopes die.

"That's how life is,"
The old men say,
"Don't fight to
Rearrange it.
Just come to terms;
Just tough it out.
You're never going
To change it."

Now theirs would be
The final word
Had we been left alone.
But Jesus Christ
Changed all of that
When He stepped
From His throne.

His cross became
A gateway
For those who'd
Dare to flee
The clutches of their
Shattered dreams
And worldling misery.

We now live to a purpose,
Lives marked by
His design,
Abounding grace
Our inner strength.
His ways are
Yours and mine.

Old men can talk
Of yesterday,
And how He took
Their sorrow.
Young men can face
Each future day
With Him who
Holds tomorrow.

Tomorrow

I entered a hospital room late one evening to find a friend, who was terminally ill, weeping softly. As I began to reassure her of our Savior's love and presence, she replied, "I know He loves me pastor, and how thankful I am to be His. But I've been lying here thinking about the way I've lived my life. I never did the really important things. It seemed I was forever taking care of insignificant details, while I promised myself that tomorrow it would be different. It never was, and now I'm here and I don't have any tomorrows left."

> If all of our tomorrows were to die,
>   And we held only fading yesterdays,
> What would they tell us of these lives of ours,
>   Of all our good intentions, works, and ways?
> Would they speak long of dreams we have not lived,
>   While cycling, rude frustrations occupy our hands,
> Or tell of interruption's ceaseless flow
>   That stole away with all our best laid plans?
> And have we waited for tomorrow's dawn—
>   The entrance of some distant time or place—
> To find fulfillment with our earthly lot
>   Where we would be content to end life's race?
> But now, with no tomorrows, hope is lost.
>   The whole of life a passing, quick parade.
> Our past but empty rounds of nothingness,
>   Turning, toiling, watching aspirations fade.

If this is what you find your life to be—

> Deign to grasp today!
>   For we may never reach tomorrow's shore
> It's what we do this moment that will mount
>   To give us all this frail life holds in store.
> Take full time for children, talk, and friends.
>   Balance labor with some measured rest.

Give yourself to acts of ministry
　　For sharing brings a sense of being blessed.
Remember, God would give His best to you.
　　Provision comes each day from Heaven's store
To grace our lives and whisper of His love,
　　And tell us that tomorrow will bring more.
So we can live here in unhurried bliss,
　　We walk with Him Who owns eternity,
We're His to order; He's to mark our way.
　　Ours to rest in Him, our Destiny.

The Divorce

America's families are being devastated by divorce. Compounding the tragedy is the fact that statistics for the Christian community are rapidly moving toward figures comparable to the national rate. An equally alarming development is found in attempts to rationalize and sell ourselves on the idea that in many cases it is a better situation for all concerned than living with problems. Too often, however, the truth tells a far different story.

"It's just not there anymore,"
He told her.
"Oh, I loved you once,
But all we do is fight.
The kids will be OK,
Better off really.
They can come on weekends,
And stay two months in the summer.
Yes, I'll support you, count on that.
Keep the house, all I want is the car.
No, there's no one else!
What kind of person do you think I am?'

He knew he was lying,
And she thought so.
With his blunt assurances
He sought to ennoble lust
And dignify his crude adultery.
It was just that, you know,
But he wouldn't find it out
Till much too late.
And when that young and supple
Flesh became common fare,
His lust would wane and barbs
Of truth set in.

The door was closed on many things that day.
For he didn't just leave a wife, you see.
It wasn't OK with the kids.
They weren't better off.
They did not endorse his leaving them—
Neither did his God.
And snatches of fatherhood in company
With a stranger
Would never salve his guilt
Or satisfy his children's needs.

When it's all over and done with,
Both of them gone from the earthly scene,
Where will the kids take theirs to remember?
There is no family place
With granite markers side by side.
There is no family.
Lust saw to that long years before.
So her remains rest here,
While his are far away.
Placed beside another—
Or maybe just alone.

The Failure

Believers do fail. All of us from time to time and in varying degrees fail the Lord—few have fallen farther than Samson, David, or Peter. And while consequences (ranging from the direct and lasting results of the transgression to God's correcting rod of chastisement) are inevitable, the good news is that He has made provision for Christians who fail.

If we confess our sins, He is faithful and just to forgive us our sins, and to cleanse us from all unrighteousness (1 Jn. 1:9).

The night can bring
    No darker thought
Than that within
    The failure wrought.

Who wreaths a family,
    Friend, and name
With emblems of
    Some public shame.

Would cause to wonder
    If could be
One such could e'er
    Forgiveness see?

Now hear the word
    Direct and true:
"I'm Savior of
    The failure too."

Then quit the place
    Of dark remorse
To find in Christ
    Life's future course.

One Nation Under God

This poem was written to commemorate our nation's bicentennial in 1976. It later received an award from the Freedom's Foundation.

Lean patriots bent their heads against the bitter
winds at Valley Forge.
With bodies wrapped in little more than rags
they sat in circles by their flickering fires and
waited for the day.
Each pondered his own future, then shared
more common thoughts of human liberty.
In great solemnity they sank on cold-numbed
knees to humbly pray—
Great God of Hosts, **preserve us.**
Let not our dream of freedom die
beneath the weight of winter's
drifting snow.
Raise Thou our hopes as Thou wilt
bring the flowers upon these meadows
come the spring.
Create in this hope-barren world
One Nation Under God.

From Philadelphia's galleries echoed forth loud
voices in prolonged debate as link by link
the chain of State was forged.
Strong men argued, reasoned, wrote, and read,
then knelt together there and softly prayed—
Great God of Hosts, **guide us.**
We are but men and need Thy wisdom
sure.
This State will not endure apart from Thee.
Be Thou our chart, our compass, and our
guiding star
that we might steer aright this
One Nation Under God.

Men stood in blue and gray to look from Appomattox
　　village across a hundred war-scarred
　　　　fields and more.
Upon them, strewn before the quiet guns,
　　reposed the silent forms of men and boys who
　　　　slept the sleep from which no man returns.
They wept, stacked rifles, cased their tattered
　　battle flags, and paused to pray—
　　　　Great God of Hosts, **unite us.**
　　　　Bind up this nation's wounds
　　　　　　and heal our hearts.
　　　　May the agonies of hate and death fast
　　　　　　be replaced by love and life from Thee,
　　　　That men might say, "She's risen again,
　　　　One Nation Under God."

In this late hour we stand to scan the past;
　　the future looms before us questioning.
Can we now forsake our fathers' way
　　and strike the face of God from off this land?
Dare we now stand mute before the Throne,
　　while full a thousand perils stalk our track?
Oh, let it not be so.
But let us bow before Him
　　low and lift a solitary voice to pray—
　　　　Great God of Hosts, **save us.**
　　　　We've strayed in shameless folly
　　　　　　far from Thee.
　　　　Mighty Lord, be quick to save us from
　　　　　　our wayward course.
　　　　Turn back our paths to truth and righteousness
　　　　　　that we might shine,
　　　　One Nation Under God!

Mother's Inner Beauty

In quiet circles by our fires we talk of strength and duty,
And contemplate how full we drank from springs of inner beauty.
It's tasted first at life's bright dawn, as infant soon discovers,
The warmth found on a silken breast in twining arms of mother.
Not only through instructive word we learn to brave the storm
But fondly patted, rocked, and held—our haven safe and warm.
She told us first how God stooped down to make man from the clay,
Of how the Christ Child came to us on manger bed of hay.
Her counsel gave us confidence when childish minds weren't sure;
Our secrets deep and questions dark were always safe with her.
She had a strength hard to define, a strength bedecked in dresses,
The kind that spoke through acts of love and motherly caresses.
Then, when the silver splashed her hair, and wrinkles creased her face,
A truth—one we had almost missed—fell firmly into place.
The best of all that she possessed was not in youthful skin,
But rather in a fountain rare that flowed from deep within.
And so we sit around our fires to talk of strength and duty,
Then thank our God that we have tasted of her inner beauty.

Christmas in July

Although it reads like pure imagination, this story actually took place up one of the quiet hollows in rural America. Some names and places have been changed and dialogue created to enhance the story. But the basic facts portrayed are indeed the facts; and the lessons, obvious and implied, are here for us all.

Time was, when having the biggest Sunday School in town was the etching on ministerial measuring sticks, and some pretty bizarre things were done in the interest of becoming number one. Dignity lost to scarfing down goldfish, catching pies in the face, or being doused with seltzer water by Bozo the Gospel Clown seemed a small price to pay when a preacher could wipe out the friendly opposition at the Monday morning ministerial meeting with attendance figures that froze conversation and provoked admiring inquiry.

Like philosophers seeking the truth, only to find it an elusive will-o'-the-wisp, numbers-conscious preachers tossed fitfully on their beds pursuing the inspiration that would birth the ultimate attendance gimmick—the really big one. Some of the less innovative, sensing they were in over their heads, went back to just inviting folk out and teaching them after they came to church.

For others, however, chasing the ultimate gimmick turned into something of an obsession. One tenacious pastor and his Sunday School superintendent finally cornered it through one of those quirkish convergences of ingenuity and accident that no one can predict or explain.

It happened over in Bent Creek, Kentucky, not far from Harlan, the county seat. Pastor Frank Macklefresh and his Sunday School Superintendent Ned Hastings were finding themselves hard pressed to rally saints to new heights and bigger numbers in Sunday School. Frankly, they were fresh out of ideas. A kind of casual desperation marked their faces as they sat in the church study sorting through strategies for a numeric breakthrough.

"You remember last year," said Ned tentatively, "that they had a Christmas in July sale down at Franklin's Five-and-Dime. I know the fellow who owns the Santa Claus suit, and I'm sure we can borrow it. Maybe we could have Christmas in July or Santa Claus Sunday, or something like that."

Pastor Frank, hands clasped behind his head, rocked back in his chair, threw a leg up on the desk, and closed his eyes. "The idea has some potential," he agreed. "But it's weak, Ned—it's been done before." He went back to thinking as Ned slumped down in his seat. No idea at all is better than a bad one, he thought.

The preacher suddenly leaped forward in his chair. "Secrecy! That's it! Total secrecy!" He spoke with an unfamiliar edge on his normally slow-gaited voice. "We can pull it off, and it may be the greatest thing we've done yet. But the key is absolute secrecy."

Ned didn't get it. A secret Sunday School promotion? The super needed to be filled in. Pastor Frank obliged.

"What we'll do," he enthused, "is have a Mystery Guest Sunday with Santa Claus as the mystery guest. We'll build suspense by dropping a new tidbit of information each week—just a teaser— use the radio, the newspaper. By the time the mystery guest is revealed, everybody in the county will want to be in on it.

"But remember, secrecy is the key. Only you and I will know. We can't even tell our wives." The reverend placed a hand on Ned's shoulder and looked him square in the eye. He held his gaze long enough to insure a proper measure of solemnity. "Ned, can I count on you to keep this secret with me?" The superintendent felt a chill ripple up the back of his neck. It was one of those moments. "You can count on me, pastor," he said, extending his hand to seal the pledge—it was about as close as a Baptist could come to swearing. Bent Creek hadn't seen such oathing to keep secrets outside the Masonic Lodge hall in decades.

Ned kept his word, and Pastor Frank worked his promotional wiles. Soon it began to spark. People started to ask questions.

Even the hard-to-impress old-timers, who perched on the bench in front of Bates Hardware, were inquisitive. "Who do you reckon the mystery guest who's comin' to the Baptist church will be?" queried Sam Arbuckle.

"Nobody knows," Bill Quincey, a member of the church, replied.

"They say the preacher won't even tell his wife who it is. I do know that Fanny Yarborough has already wasted three or four chicken dinners tryin' to weasel it out of the preacher. All he'll say is it's somebody who's recognized all over the world and a face known to every American."

"Sounds like a pretty big fish for Bent Creek, if you ask me," snapped old man Catlett.

As the weeks went by, and suspense built, Pastor Frank's optimism soared. "This," he confided to Ned, "will be the best one yet. It just feels so right."

No doubt about it, it was big and getting bigger. But, in all honesty, without the entrance of an unprogrammed windfall, it probably wouldn't have reached "big one" status.

It came like a bolt out of the blue—an accident—a pure freak of history. But it fell with the brilliance of a giant meteor and caused Mystery Guest Sunday to explode as nothing had in the craggy hollows of Harlan County. Pastor Frank and Ned Hastings were three weeks away from promotional immortality.

The Bates Hardware bench sitters were passing comments on news from the *Daily Harlantonian* when Scrawny Wilson spoke up. "See where Harry Truman is coming to Harlan."

Catlett wanted to know what on earth the former President of the United States would be doing in their part of the country.

Scrawny read on. "He's comin' to speak at the dedication of the new federal building. The Democrats want to squeeze all the publicity they can out of that ugly pile of bricks."

"Well, I guess the crowd over at the courthouse will be there to bow down," said another militant Republican with no little sarcasm in his voice.

"What about the grommet factory bunch?" tossed in another. "They haven't hired a Republican since Henry Tuttle was fired for painting a beard on F.D.R.'s picture."

"Maybe they won't have to go to Harlan," Scrawny observed with a suggestive tilt of his head. "He'll be there the same weekend as the mystery guest is comin' to Bent Creek Baptist. Maybe old Harry is the mystery guest."

His tongue-in-cheek remark had been made in jest. But the mere mention of a name like Harry S. Truman in Bent Creek, Kentucky, was enough to encourage serious conversation. The feisty ex-President was a symbol of the kind of shoot-from-the-hip independence so revered by people in those parts. So when Scrawny's comment began to circulate, it didn't take long for the local rumor mill to refine and embellish the remark.

It was all so natural. Truman was a Baptist. He had to go to church somewhere that weekend. And hadn't Pastor Frank dropped hints in sermons from time to time fostering the conclusion that he had connections way up the ladder in Washington? Sure they'd have to keep it a secret. Think of all the trouble it would cause if the big churches in the state found out they'd been bypassed for Bent Creek.

Mrs. Yarborough hadn't moved so fast in thirty years. She could hardly contain herself until the pastor's wife answered her persistent ringing of the doorbell.

"Now Nancy," she said insistently, "I know Pastor Frank wouldn't leave you in the dark about this mystery guest thing. Tell me right out, is it Harry Truman?"

Nancy flushed with embarrassment. But before she was forced to reveal her ignorance, the sound of the pastor's key in the front door got her off the hook.

Now Fanny Yarborough was not a talebearer to be trifled with. She had more devices for extracting information than the town's grommet factory had grommets.

"I've heard the rumors," she began, eyeing Pastor Frank carefully. "We have a pretty good idea who the mystery guest is going to be. It is Harry Truman, isn't it?" Her hatchet-chop, get-right-to-the-heart-of-things approach had been constructed to at least evoke a telltale flutter of the eyes that would give the secret away.

The preacher didn't flinch. "Sorry," he answered with an exaggerated shrug of his shoulders. "I'm afraid I have been pledged to secrecy. Believe me, I would really like to tell you, but I'm simply not at liberty to say anything before the third Sunday in July."

Mrs. Y was busy putting two and two together while Frank was speaking. "Not at liberty to say"? "Pledged to secrecy"? She concluded it must have something to do with the Secret Service. That almost clinched it.

"Well, pastor, you know I'm a person who can keep a secret. And I am not here out of idle curiosity—far from it. If the mystery guest turns out to be who we think it is, as president of the Social Committee it is my duty to prepare a proper reception. I can understand the need for secrecy under these circumstances, but it wouldn't hurt you to drop just one little hint."

Pastor Frank was almost whispering. "All I can say is what you've already heard: His is a name known the world over; his is a face known to every American."

"His" was a new insertion into the phrase she had listened to every Sunday, and innumerable times in between, over the past several weeks. It was what she had been looking for. He hadn't said it in so many words, but there it was—plain as the nose on your face: Harry S. Truman was coming to Bent Creek!

As the door closed behind her, Frank roared with laughter and reached for Nancy's shoulder. To his surprise, she twisted away and bounded off toward the kitchen. "Come on now, honey," he consoled. "You have to be a good sport about this." Nancy Macklefresh was in no mood to be a "good sport," and things were very quiet at the minister's table that evening. The silence would thicken as the days passed.

The parson smiled into the darkness from his pillow that night. Nancy would understand everything when the big day came. Until then, he would have to travel the lonely road trod by fellow immortals who were forced to keep their own counsel. But, my, how he was enjoying the journey.

Mystery Guest Sunday dawned clear and pleasant over their excited corner of the world. As was his custom, Pastor Frank was at the radio station early for his weekly "Breakfast with the Baptists" program.

"Well folks, Mystery Guest Sunday is finally here, and I can't tell you what a relief it is for yours truly, Pastor Frank, and the staff over at the church. Phone lines have been jammed for weeks, and we've all been busy answering letters and questions you people have been asking.

"Now I know some of you can't be with us today because you will be in your own church or at home as a shut-in. So in the true spirit of ecumenicity, we are going to let everybody in on the secret the minute our mystery guest's identity is known.

"I have here in my hand a sealed envelope with the name of our special visitor safe inside. I am now placing it in the care of your announcer here at the station." The morning D.J., who was lounging behind the Sunday funnies on the other side of the studio window, threw a casual but confident thumbs-up toward the preacher.

"At precisely 12:00 noon, he will open the envelope and reveal the name of the mystery guest."

After the broadcast—it was a glorious morning—the pastor strode into the sunlight. He got into his car and wheeled away toward the church, anxious to get there and survey the full effects of his magnificent deception.

When he was two blocks away, Frank found the streets lined with people hurrying toward the church. He parked his car, followed the crowd, and slipped in through the side door.

The preacher couldn't explain it, but, all at once, he was gripped with an acute feeling that something was desperately wrong. The sensation was aggravated when he peeked into the auditorium through the choir door. Floor-to-ceiling, wall-to-wall, the place was jammed—every seat taken, with people standing two deep against the walls. The mayor was seated alongside the police chief. Volunteer fire fighters and rescue squad members, in full regalia, had commandeered two full pews. Bent Creek's newspaper editor and assorted dignitaries were scattered about the building. Silas Burton, *The Bent Creek Chronicle's* ace reporter and photographer, was strategically placed, center-front, camera at the ready, waiting for things to get started. Beyond them all was a vestibule full of eager bodies. Those bodies were expecting to see, hear, and perhaps even press the flesh of a living American legend—Harry S. Truman. Clearly, Santa Claus just wasn't going to make the grade.

A smitten Pastor Frank backed into the hall, turned, and started for the study. He was beginning to feel gravely ill.

"You've done it this time preacher," crowed an usher as he hurried by gripping a handful of visitor's cards and extra offering plates.

A deflated minister fell into the chair where the idea had been hatched. His wonderful and innovative stroke of promotional genius had suddenly become a volcano erupting in the pit of his stomach and sending excruciating streams of fiery anxiety to all parts of his body. Words like *duplicity*, *betrayer of the trusting*, *deceiver*, *hoodwinker*, and *stupid* were thumping his head.

Somewhere, he was reasonably sure, old give-'em-thunder Harry was bounding, jut-jawed, up the front steps of a Baptist church. Somewhere, a smiling pastor was extending a hand of welcome to the former head of state. But that church was not Bent Creek Baptist, and Frank Macklefresh was definitely not the favored pastor. What he would give, he thought, if by some miracle of providence H. S. Truman would have walked through the door of his church.

Ned came in without knocking. He was nearly beside himself. "We're all ready," he announced grandly, the other half of the "we're" being Artus, the third essential conspirator.

Pastor and Ned had waited until the last minute and then talked their way through a host of rejects before settling on Artus as the perfect mystery guest. He was a man who had never asked a question in his life and enjoyed everything he did, whether he understood it or not.

"Where's Artus?" asked the subdued preacher.

"Don't worry. He's in a Sunday School room out back. I put newspapers over the windows so nobody could look in. We stuffed some rags down in the Santa suit so he could have a good fit. Artus is having the time of his life.

"I haven't told you this, but I've added something. I have a bag full of candy canes for him to throw out to the people when he comes in. I thought it would be a nice touch. He's a little weak on his 'Ho! Ho! Ho's!' but I think they will be able to hear him all right."

"You know, Ned, I've been thinking," said the pastor who was trying hard to look calm. "This whole thing is really a Sunday School project. I think it only fitting that you introduce the mystery guest. I'll be on the platform, but you do the honors."

He knew it was a gutless thing to do. But at that moment Frank Macklefresh was a consummately gutless man—one who was struggling mightily with an aggressive urge to leave the premises.

For his part, Ned was deeply moved. This was undoubtedly the biggest moment in the century-long history of Bent Creek Baptist Church, and the moment would be his.

After an abbreviated introduction by the pastor, oddly devoid of any acknowledgement of visiting dignitaries, Ned stepped forward. He had prepared meticulously. With opening remarks fashioned to heighten suspense, he edged toward the object of the occasion. As he swung into the final phases of the unveiling, people strained forward in their seats. The photographer from the paper took his place, camera poised, on one knee in the center of the aisle.

"And now," Ned called out lyrically, "the moment we've all been waiting for. Here he is . . . our special mystery guest . . . the one . . . the only . . . Santa Claus!"

Artus leaped through the door and pranced around on the platform bombarding the audience with discordant "Ho! Ho! Ho's!" Red and green candy cane missiles flew in all directions. Nobody caught them. Nobody did anything. They just stared, open-mouthed, in leaden silence.

Little Sarah Jennings squirmed through the inert bodies and out the side door. She was making a beeline toward the public phone across the street from church. Sarah was obeying dad's orders to a tee. Her father, a supervisor at the grommet factory, had been forced to pull duty on the big day. His compensation would be announcing the identity of the mystery guest over the loud speaker system to busy fellow grommet makers. His daughter's sole responsibility was to relay the celebrity's name.

"Hello, daddy. This is Sarah."

"Yes, honey."

"The mystery guest is here."

"Who is it?"

"Santa Claus."

"Sarah! This is no time to fool around. Who is the mystery guest?"

"It was Santa Claus. Honest. I think he's gone now."

The silence chilling the auditorium at Bent Creek Baptist now froze the telephone wire between Main Street and the grommet factory. In the first visible reaction to the event, Henry Jennings sneaked out the rear door of the factory and went home. People left the church in the same manner and mood.

Nancy knocked softly on the study door. Receiving no answer, she entered. Frank was crouching over his desk writing. The first word fighting to leap from her mouth was *Why?* She managed to stifle it, however, in favor of a choice better suited to the moment.

"What are you doing, dear?" "I'm writing my resignation, that's what I'm doing. We're getting out of this town as soon as we can."

The deacons, aware of their shepherd's snap decision, were holding the first secret board meeting at Bent Creek in over fifty years. Two resolutions were entertained.

1) Pastor Frank's resignation would not be accepted.

2) The deacons would hear no criticism from the congregation about Mystery Guest Sunday.

Frank didn't want to see it come, but it was inevitable—Monday always is. He arrived at the church a little early—without witnesses, he hoped. The church office, which had always been such a happy place, appeared somehow empty and downright cold—sort of like Christmas would be from then on.

He sat in unbroken solitude until midmorning, when the secretary reluctantly stuck her head in. She didn't usually work on Mondays, but the chairman of the board had asked her to come in and field calls.

"The editor of the paper is on the phone," she said, almost apologetically. "Do you want to speak with him?"

"Do I have a choice?" he moaned as his hand slid toward the receiver.

"Preacher, I thought you'd like to know about the staff meeting we had this morning on what happened at the church yesterday." The newsman waited for a reaction, but the preacher didn't respond.

"We've decided, if you don't mind, not to run the feature story we'd planned on your mystery guest. He'll get plenty of coverage in a few months.

"Oh, yes, we have a half-dozen eight-by-ten glossies of the mystery guest I'm going to send over in a few minutes. We thought you'd appreciate the look on your face while Santa was on stage."

The call broke the tension, and the town began to laugh at what had taken place. It took Pastor Frank considerably longer to find any humor in the grand catastrophe. But he finally did, and the lessons he and Bent Creek Baptist learned made the whole episode almost—only almost—worthwhile.

Risen With Him
2 Thessalonians 4:13-18

Soon Christ will come
   To call His Church—His own,
Who often walk their earthly paths
   Aweary and alone.

And what a glad transition
   We who are His shall know,
Arrayed in heavenly vestments
   That pale the driven snow.

But, oh, the thought most glorious,
   It guides us through the fray:
We'll join our risen Savior
   On resurrection day.